101 Easy Supper Ideas

*A Smorgasbord of Recipes and
Inspiration for Busy Moms*

Ellyn Sanna

PROMISE
PRESS

© 2001 by Ellyn Sanna

ISBN 1-58660-144-X

All rights reserved. No part of this publication may be reproduced or transmitted in any form or by any means without written permission of the publisher.

All Scripture quotations, unless otherwise indicated, are taken from the HOLY BIBLE, NEW INTERNATIONAL VERSION®. NIV®. Copyright © 1973, 1978, 1984 by International Bible Society. Used by permission of Zondervan Publishing House. All rights reserved.

Scripture quotations marked KJV are taken from the King James Version of the Bible.

Scripture quotations marked NKJV are taken from the New King James Version. Copyright © 1979, 1980, 1982 by Thomas Nelson, Inc. Used by permission. All rights reserved.

Scripture quotations marked TLB are taken from *The Living Bible* copyright © 1971. Used by permission of Tyndale House Publishers, Inc., Wheaton, Illinois 60189. All rights reserved.

Scripture quotations marked NLT are taken from the *Holy Bible,* New Living Translation, copyright © 1996. Used by permission of Tyndale House Publishers, Inc. Wheaton, Illinois 60189, U.S.A. All rights reserved.

Published by Promise Press, an imprint of Barbour Publishing, Inc., P.O. Box 719, Uhrichsville, Ohio 44683, http://www.promispress.com

Member of the
Evangelical Christian
Publishers Association

Printed in the United States of America.

Contents

The Challenge:

Finding Time to Cook,
Finding Time for God

We cannot control all the factors of our lives;
we can only toss the busy pieces up into God's waiting hands.
ELLYN SANNA,
Motherhood: A Spiritual Journey

Motherhood's Juggling Act

There's just not enough time in the day for everything. That's why, as mothers, all of us juggle. We juggle jobs and roles and a hundred tiny little chores. On any given day, we are not only responsible for the emotional well-being of our families, the physical upkeep of our homes, and the laundry, but many of us are also the ones who answer the phone, keep track of the social calendars for several people, walk the dog, pay the bills, help out with homework—*and* figure out what to have for supper. No wonder we end up talking over a friend's problem on the phone while we fold laundry, quizzing our kids on their spelling words while we brush our teeth, and communicating weekend plans with our husbands while we pack lunches. We're always doing at least two things at the same time, and our juggling routines can get pretty frantic. We may even drop a few balls.

As the balls begin to fly away, you will instinctively try to pick them up.
Turning this way and that, lunging, reaching, grabbing forward and
back at the bounding spheres, you may find yourself lurching
in more dircections than you ever thought existed.

STEVE COHEN, *Just Juggle*

Keeping Christ at the Center

When our lives are so busy, how do we make time for God? As mothers, we have so many people counting on us. Scrambling to catch all those bouncing balls, sometimes we're just too busy, just too tired, to spend much time with Jesus. We need Him desperately—and yet our relationship with Him may seem like yet another ball we have to somehow keep up in the air. And when we don't, when other aspects of our busy lives distract us from this one shining ball, we may feel guilty and ashamed.

When I first started writing and talking to mothers about the juggling act we all play, I looked at juggling simply as a word picture for the frustration of a mother's life. After all, I thought, who would *choose* to juggle so many different things all at the same time? How much nicer it would be, I reasoned, to simply have one ball to toss easily and perfectly up and down, up and down, never missing or dropping it. If my life was like that, I thought, surely I could live in a way that would be wholly pleasing to God. But as I read about the actual physical art of juggling objects, I realized that what I had seen as a metaphor for frustration could also provide me with an image of hope.

A juggler, I discovered, takes many separate elements and combines them into one unified whole; a juggler creates a pattern in the midst of chaos. She does this not by focusing on each ball as it falls into her hand, but by keeping her focus beyond the individual balls.

How does this apply to my life as a mother? Well, when I look at juggling from this perspective, I realize all the separate roles and responsibilities that fill my life are actually part of something bigger. And as it turns out, my relationship with

God is not merely one piece of my juggling act. Instead, each of my roles, all the spinning pieces of my life, combine to form who I am in relationship to God. My connection to Him through Jesus is the pattern that makes sense of everything else. And when I keep my focus on Him, rather than on the immediate responsibility of each moment, then He helps me see the pattern in my seemingly chaotic life.

Yes, I still need to make a specific time for God in the midst of my busy days. But spending time with Him is not just one item to be checked off my long to-do list. Instead, I can offer my entire life to Him, including even the most hectic moments. When I do, making lunches, doing the laundry, running errands, snuggling my children, cooking suppers, all become a prayer. I find His presence with me through each busy moment.

If a juggler were to focus on each individual ball, she would quickly lose her rhythm. Focusing on the ball she'd just released, she would miss the ball about to fall into her hand; anticipating the ball that was coming, she'd drop the one she has. I find all too often I do the same in my life. I spend my energy worrying over what I just did, fretting about all I have to do next, and my focus on the bigger picture disappears. Trying so hard to juggle perfectly, I lose sight of God. But when I turn to Christ throughout my day, opening my heart to Him, then He has room to live at the center of my life. His presence makes sense out of my life's chaos.

That doesn't mean I necessarily begin to juggle with miraculous efficiency and grace. But when Christ is the focal point of my juggling act, then my own success or failure is not important, for His grace will see me through. "When I am weak, then I am strong," Paul says in 2 Corinthians 12, because Christ's "power is made perfect in weakness." If we could do everything perfectly, all by ourselves, then we wouldn't need to rely on God.

So as a mother who juggles many things, I need to quickly let go of each moment's responsibility, tossing it up into God's waiting hands. In practical terms, I remind myself to do this by simply whispering, "Into Your hands, Lord," throughout my day—or even simply, "Yours, Lord." If instead, though, I try to clutch each responsibility tight, reluctant to trust God to catch it, then my hands are too full to catch the other balls that begin to bounce around me on the floor. As a juggler, I have to let go of my life moment by moment. That's what faith is all about: learning to let go, learning to trust God to juggle with me.

What does that mean when it comes to cooking supper for my family? What does faith have to do with the daily kitchen routine? Is God interested in something as mundane as what we have for supper?

Well, actually, I think God is very interested in what goes on in our kitchens and around our tables. He loves us and no detail in our lives is too small for His concern. As you use this book, you'll find it is chock-full of Scripture references to food and eating, and the Bible holds even more than I've included here.

In His Word, God makes clear that food is an important symbol for His kingdom. After all, think about the time when Jesus fed the five thousand. . . .

That evening the disciples came to him and said,
"This is a desolate place, and it is getting late. Send the crowds away. . . ."
But Jesus replied, "That isn't necessary—you feed them."
"Impossible!" they exclaimed. "We have only five loaves of bread and two fish!"
"Bring them here," he said. . . . And he took the five loaves and two fish,
looked up toward heaven, and asked God's blessing on the food. . . .
They all ate as much as they wanted, and they picked up twelve baskets of leftovers.
About five thousand men had eaten from those five loaves,
in addition to all the women and children.
MATTHEW 14:15–21 NLT

Good,

the more communicated,

the more abundant grows.

JOHN MILTON

I have to confess that some days I juggle more smoothly than others. Some days, quite frankly, I find this juggling act I play frustrating, not to mention exhausting. On those days, suppertime always seems to be the low point in my day. The kids are cranky, my husband's still at work, and I've spent all my stores of creativity and patience. On top of all that, I'm hungry. I want someone to feed *me*—and instead I have to scrape together a meal for my family.

That being the case, I won't pretend to be the personification of Betty Crocker. And I won't claim to be the well-organized and triumphant patron saint of time management, someone who has all the answers. The truth is, as the family cook, I'm not always a shining model of efficiency and creativity.

Which is why I depend on the recipes in this book. They are 101 tried and true friends I can depend on, no matter how hectic my juggling routine has been that day. These recipes, combined with a little forethought, are what stand between my family and a lifetime of takeout meals.

I hope you'll find these recipes help your own juggling act go a little more smoothly as well.

The time of business does not with me differ from the time of prayer;
and in the noise and clatter of my kitchen,
while several persons are at the same time calling for different things,
I possess God in as great tranquility as if I were on my knees.
BROTHER LAWRENCE

Planning for the Nightly Dilemma:

Casseroles and Other Oven-Baked Meals

Mothering has always been an exhausting life
(think about a world without washers, dryers, or permanent press;
without vaccines, antibiotics, or Tylenol;
without grocery stores, refrigerators, or sliced bread). . . .
The challenge is tremendous.
Motherhood is no soft, warm place where we can curl up and relax.
Instead it is a journey that requires hard work.

ELLYN SANNA,
Motherhood: A Spiritual Journey

101 Easy Supper Ideas

$\mathcal{S}$ometimes I feel guilty that my meals don't live up to those I remember my mother preparing when I was a child. And they certainly don't measure up to my grandmother's. When I have so many time-saving devices and modern conveniences, why is it so hard to find the time for everything I need to accomplish in a day?

Recently, though, I leafed through a 1950s "time-management" book for mothers. The author recommended that mothers follow this schedule:

Monday: housecleaning
Tuesday: laundry and ironing
Wednesday: Bible study group/other social gatherings
Thursday: letter writing
Friday: menu planning, groceries, errands
Saturday: baking
Sunday: church and family

I don't know about you—but my life isn't quite that simple. (I certainly don't have a day a week I can devote to writing letters!) But if my life were simpler, if I weren't juggling quite so fast, I could certainly do a better job at planning and preparing meals.

Given the busy circumstances of our lives, we're all doing the best we can.

But even if we can't devote entire days to one activity like our mothers and grandmothers may have, making a plan does help. By thinking ahead, we can avoid that desperate moment at 5:30 every evening when we realize it's suppertime and we have nothing in the house to cook.

Since we have five people in our family, I sometimes let each person pick a

JUGGLING TIP:
Once a week, sit down and make a week's worth of menus. Use this as the basis for your grocery list.

menu for each of the five weeknights; that way, at least one person is always happy at suppertime. And I don't have to do all of the decision making.

The casserole recipes that follow are good for plan-ahead meals. Make double each time you prepare a recipe, and freeze half for another night. If you know you have a stressful week ahead, prepare a bunch of these meals on the weekend and then all you have to do is heat them up. They're easy, hearty, and nourishing.

Enjoy!

WILD RICE TURKEY MEDLEY

3 cups cooked wild rice
3 cups chopped cooked turkey
1 (16-oz) package frozen
    French-cut green beans, thawed
½ cup dried bread crumbs
2 tbsp butter, melted

½ cup chopped red pepper
    (or 1- or 2-oz jar chopped
    pimiento, undrained)
1 (17-oz) jar prepared Alfredo
    sauce

Heat oven to 350°. Place wild rice, turkey, green beans, and red pepper in 12x8-inch ungreased baking dish. Pour sauce over top. In a small bowl, stir together bread crumbs and butter; sprinkle over casserole. Bake 45 to 50 minutes, or until heated through and mixture is bubbly at edges. Makes 6 servings.

Thou shalt accomplish my desire,
in giving food for my household.
1 KINGS 5:9 KJV

Lord, help me to depend on You
as I prepare my family's meals.

SAUSAGE AND APPLE STRATA

8 egg whites
4 whole eggs
1½ cups low-fat (1%) milk
2 tbsp Dijon mustard
½ tsp salt
½ tsp black pepper
6 slices multigrain bread, cubed

8 oz precooked reduced-fat
   turkey sausage, removed
   from casings and crumbled
½ tsp dried sage
2 Granny Smith apples, peeled, cored,
   and cut into ½-inch cubes
1½ cups shredded cheddar cheese (6 oz)

Spray 13x9x2-inch baking pan with nonstick cooking spray. In a small bowl, lightly beat together egg whites and whole eggs; stir in milk, mustard, salt, and pepper. Combine bread, sausage, and sage in large bowl. Place in baking pan. Layer apples next, then pour egg mixture evenly over all. Sprinkle cheese over top and cover with foil. Let stand 10 minutes, or may be prepared ahead and refrigerated for up to 10 hours. Bake, covered, at 425° for 10 minutes; uncover and bake for 15 minutes more, or until top is lightly browned. Let stand for 10 minutes. Goes well with a tossed green salad. 6 servings.

*And out of the ground made the LORD God to grow every tree
that is pleasant to the sight, and good for food.*
GENESIS 2:9 KJV

**Remind us, God,
that You delight in giving us good things.**

CHILI RELLENOS SQUARES

1 lb lean ground beef
²/₃ cup salsa
¹/₂ cup water
1 cup uncooked instant rice
8 oz (2 cups) cheddar cheese, shredded
¹/₂ tsp salt

1 (4-oz) can chopped green
    chiles, undrained
1 cup milk
¹/₃ cup all-purpose flour
4 eggs

Heat oven to 350°. In a 10-inch skillet, cook ground beef over medium-high heat 6 to 7 minutes or until browned. Drain off fat. Add salsa and water, and continue cooking 4 to 5 minutes, or until mixture comes to a boil. Spray 8-inch square baking dish with nonstick cooking spray. Place rice in dish. Spread meat mixture evenly over rice; sprinkle with half of cheese, chiles, and then remaining cheese. Beat together milk, flour, eggs, and salt; pour over cheese. Bake, uncovered, for 35 to 40 minutes, or until knife inserted near center comes out clean. Allow to stand 5 minutes; cut and serve. Makes 6 servings.

*Here you can have intimate communion with Christ and feast on his love;
here are tables well-stored with food for you to live on for ever. . .*

CHARLES SPURGEON

**Jesus, as I feed my family,
may I never be too busy to feast on Your love.**

Unconditional Love

If you're a mother, then I'm fairly certain that meal preparation is one of the elements of life you struggle to keep "up in the air." Yes, many men also cook (my husband is one of them), and as children grow older they can be taught to take over more and more of the family chores that circle around mealtimes. But no matter how helpful your family is, chances are at least some, if not most, of the responsibility for meals falls squarely on your shoulders. Sometimes that responsibility can feel pretty heavy. It's hard to keep all the other elements of our lives spinning smoothly around our heads when three times a day we have to stop what we're doing and think about food.

Oftentimes, though, it's the little voices inside our own heads that make our juggling acts so taxing on our emotional, spiritual, and physical strength. These voices whisper that we have to be perfect at everything we do, that we have to measure up to the expectations of everyone around us at all times, that we will somehow be more "worthy" of God's love if we can do everything smoothly and competently and. . .well, perfectly.

> THE LORD
> DELIGHTETH
> IN THEE.
> ISAIAH 62:4 KJV

Let's get something straight, though, before we go any further: God is not calling us to be perfect. He loves us just as much no matter how messy our kitchens are, and we are equally precious in His sight when we serve our children take-out as when we serve them a well-balanced meal based on the nutritional requirements of the food pyramid. God wants us to drop that load of guilt we've been trying to keep up in the air along with all the other things we're juggling. The little voice that whispers we have to be perfect is really the enemy of our souls.

Yes, putting supper on the table over and over day after day can drain our patience and creativity. That's why books like this one are written: to give us some practical suggestions and recipes we can use when our ideas are all used up. The recipes in this book will provide you with 101 easy meals that will make your life a little simpler.

That may make you happier. It may make your family happier. But it won't make God love you any more than He does already.

You provide delicious food for me in the presence of my enemies. You have welcomed me as your guest; blessings overflow!

PSALM 23:5 TLB

HEARTY SALMON PIE

CRUST
½ cup butter
½ cup finely crushed, dried, crumbly-style herb-seasoned stuffing

FILLING
2 cups crushed, dried, crumbly-style herb-seasoned stuffing
1 cup water
½ cup milk
1 (14½-oz) can red salmon, drained, skin and bones removed, flaked (or three 6-oz cans tuna, drained and flaked)

4 oz (1 cup) cheddar cheese, shredded
2 eggs
2 tbsp chopped fresh parsley
1 tbsp finely chopped onion
½ tsp dry mustard

SAUCE
½ cup sour cream
½ cup mayonnaise

1 tbsp dried dill weed
fresh dill sprigs, if desired

Heat oven to 350°. Spray 9-inch deep-dish pie plate with cooking spray. In 3-quart saucepan melt ½ cup butter; stir in ½ cup finely crushed stuffing. Press stuffing mixture into prepared pie plate; set aside. Mix filling ingredients together in saucepan; pour onto crust. Bake 43 to 48 minutes, or until heated through. Let stand 10 minutes. Stir sauce ingredients together in medium-sized bowl; cover and refrigerate until serving time. Cut into wedges to serve; top with sauce and garnish with fresh dill. Makes 6 servings.

The wilderness yieldeth food for them and for their children.
JOB 24:5 KJV

Even on the wildest days, God, I know You will provide for us.

CHICKEN AND RICE BAKE

2 cups frozen broccoli cuts
2 cups water
½ cup sliced water chestnuts,
   drained
1 (6-oz) package wild and
   white rice mix

4 (5-oz) boneless, skinless
   chicken breast halves
1 cup sour cream
1 tbsp Dijon-style mustard
½ cup sliced almonds
1 tbsp butter, melted

Heat oven to 350°. In an 8-inch square baking dish, combine broccoli, water, water chestnuts, and rice mix. Place chicken breasts on top; cover with foil and bake until most of liquid is absorbed (about 50 minutes). Stir to push center rice to edges (remove chicken breasts if necessary). Replace chicken breasts on rice. Mix sour cream and mustard; spread evenly over chicken breasts. Stir together almonds and butter; sprinkle over sour cream mixture and bake for another 10 to 15 minutes, or until topping is lightly browned. Makes 4 servings.

Bread shall be given him; his waters shall be sure.
ISAIAH 33:16 KJV

**Remind me, Lord, that my family is dependent on
Your strength and providence.**

BARBECUE BEEF & BEAN CASSEROLE

1 lb ground beef
1 medium (½ cup) onion, chopped
4 slices bacon, chopped
½ cup firmly packed brown sugar
½ cup ketchup
1 tbsp prepared mustard
1 cup crushed corn chips

1 tbsp vinegar
1 (16-oz) can baked beans
1 (14½-oz) can yellow wax beans, drained
1 (8-oz) can green beans, drained
4 oz (1 cup) American cheese, shredded

Heat oven to 375°. Place ground beef, onion, and bacon in 10-inch skillet. Brown over medium heat for 5 to 8 minutes, stirring occasionally. Drain off fat. Combine ground beef mixture and next 7 ingredients in a 3-quart casserole. Bake until heated through and bubbly around edges (about 50 to 60 minutes). Sprinkle with crushed corn chips and cheese. Bake for an additional 5 to 6 minutes until cheese is melted. Makes 6 servings.

O give thanks unto the LORD; for he is good. . . .
Who giveth food to all flesh: for his mercy endureth for ever.
PSALM 136:1, 25 KJV

Thank You, Lord, for Your enduring mercy.

Up to Jesus

When they got home, if they ever did, Leah would have so much work to do. All the cooking to get ready for the evening meal, and with the Sabbath tomorrow, food preparation had to be done before sunset. . . . She shifted her weight and sighed.

Her husband Jacob had been listening to this strange Man talk ever since this morning, but Leah could barely hear the Man's voice, and she was too short to even catch a glimpse of Him over the heads of the crowd. But when she looked up at her husband's face, hoping to catch his eye so he would know she was ready to go home, she saw that his face was full of eager light, as though he were listening to some wonderful news he had been longing all his life to hear. Leah felt a twinge of envy. . .and then her thoughts shifted back to the cooking she needed to do when they got back home.

The sun was far past the midpoint in the sky now; how could she possibly get everything done before sunset? Her mind worried the problem back and forth, the way their dog liked to chew a piece of old leather. At least she had packed them all a nice lunch this morning, the bread and fish both fresh and good, but they had eaten their lunches hours ago now, and why, oh why, couldn't the Man just stop talking so they could all go home? She had plenty of dried meat, as well as the figs from their tree, and there was the cheese. . .but it wouldn't be enough for both tonight's meal and tomorrow. . .

Isaac came dancing through the crowd and interrupted her thoughts. "Mother, I went right up to Him! He smiled at me. Mother, can I—"

She nodded, too preoccupied to really hear her son's chatter. Maybe the bread she had baked this morning would be enough for tomorrow if they ate only a little fruit and cheese tonight. Her stomach growled so loudly, she barely heard the crowd begin to murmur.

"Did you hear that?" Jacob asked her.

"I can't hear anything," she said crossly. "I don't know how *you* can. We might as well go home, don't you think?" She looked up at him hopefully.

"They're going to feed us here," Jacob said. "If they can. Everyone is hungry, and His disciples are asking us all to share whatever we have left from our lunches."

"Oh, let's just go home. Everyone will have eaten their lunches long ago." If they left now, she might have time to make some stew. . .

Isaac interrupted her thoughts again. "Mother!" He pulled on her sleeve. "I didn't eat my lunch. I had a stomachache, remember? I was just going to ask you if I could eat it now." He turned to his father. "Can I give it to them?"

"Can't we just go home?" Leah whispered to Jacob. But he had already nodded and Isaac had dashed off through the crowd. Leah sighed again. "That little bit of food won't do this crowd any good. And I have so much work to do when we get home. All that cooking for tonight and tomorrow. . . Please. Let's go."

Jacob looked over the crowd toward the Man Who stood at the center. "I'd like to think we gave Him whatever we had, Leah. Even if it's only five loaves and a couple of fish."

As he spoke, a hush fell across the people, and then everyone began to sit down. Isaac wormed his way back to them, his face ablaze with excitement. "My lunch is the only food they have. But the Man blessed it, and now they're passing it out. They're sharing it with everyone."

"How silly," Leah started to say, and then someone handed her a generous portion of bread and fish. She looked down at it; she looked at the bread and fish in the hands of everyone around her; she tasted a bit of the fish and sniffed the bread. It was hers: the same food she had prepared this morning.

And then, at last, over the heads of the crowd, she caught a glimpse of the Man's face. He looked straight at her and smiled. She'd been so worried about the cooking when all this time. . .

Tears sprang to her eyes. "I don't understand."

Jacob touched her face. "It's all right. I think all we have to do is give Him what we have. Even on the days when we don't have very much. The rest is up to Him."

My grace is sufficient for you.

2 CORINTHIANS 12:9

Bacon, Potato, and Onion Frittata

4 strips lean bacon, cut in ½-inch pieces
½ lb small red potatoes, thinly sliced
1 large red onion, chopped
1 tbsp chopped fresh rosemary or
   1 tsp dried rosemary
6 eggs

3 tbsp water
½ tsp salt
½ tsp ground black pepper
½ tsp ground paprika
fresh rosemary sprig for
   garnish (optional)

Heat oven to 350°. In nonstick skillet with ovenproof handle,* brown bacon pieces for 5 minutes. Place on paper towel to drain; reserve 1 tbsp fat in skillet and add potato, onion, and rosemary. Cover and cook over low heat until tender (about 10 minutes), turning slices. Whisk eggs, water, salt, and pepper in a bowl. Pour over potatoes, stir in bacon, and sprinkle with paprika. Bake, uncovered, for 8 to 10 minutes or until set. Garnish with rosemary if desired. Makes 4 servings.

Wrap nonovenproof skillet handle tightly in foil.

Praise the Lord. . .which giveth food to the hungry.
Psalm 146:1, 7 kjv

**When my heart is as hungry as my family's stomachs,
Lord, remind me to praise You even then,
knowing that You will nourish me.**

CHUNKY CHICKEN POTPIE

1 (19-oz) can kidney beans
1 (4.5-oz) jar sliced mushrooms
3 cups diced cooked chicken
1 (10.75-oz) can condensed cream
  of chicken soup
1 (4-oz) can diced green chiles, drained
½ cup water
1 egg mixed with 1 tbsp water

½ tsp dried sage
½ tsp dried thyme
½ tsp salt
⅛ tsp black pepper
1 sheet frozen puff pastry
  (from 17.25-oz package),
  thawed
1 tbsp grated Parmesan cheese

Heat oven to 400°. Drain beans and mushrooms; rinse beans. Mix beans and mushrooms with chicken, soup, chiles, water, sage, thyme, salt, and pepper in a large bowl. Pour into an 8x8x2-inch glass baking dish. Gently layer pastry on top of filling; crimp edges along rim to seal. Using a brush, coat pastry with egg-water mixture; sprinkle with Parmesan cheese. Cut ten 1-inch steam vents in pastry. Bake for 30 minutes, covering with aluminum foil if crust browns too quickly. Let stand for 10 minutes before serving. Makes 6 servings.

And our fellowship is with the Father and with his Son, Jesus Christ.

1 JOHN 1:3

***Tonight as we eat supper, Lord,
may we also fellowship with You.***

TEX-MEX MEAT LOAF

2 eggs
2½ lbs ground beef
1½ cups bottled salsa
75 whole (3 to 4 cups) lower-fat, nacho-flavored, baked tortilla chips, finely ground
    (about 1½ cups)
½ cup packaged unseasoned dry breadcrumbs
½ tsp salt
1 cup shredded taco-flavored cheese
salsa, avocado slices, and shredded, taco-flavored cheese (optional)

Heat oven to 350°. Place eggs in a large bowl; beat slightly. Combine ground beef, 1 cup salsa, ground chips, bread crumbs, salt, and half the cheese; mix well. Pour into 9x5x3-inch loaf pan and pat firmly into shape. Bake for 1 hour. Spread remaining salsa and cheese over meat loaf and bake an additional 15 minutes. Let stand for 10 minutes. Pour off grease and slice on cutting board. Serve with additional salsa and garnish with avocado and cheese, if desired. Makes 10 servings.

Bread I broke with you was more than bread.
CONRAD AIKEN

**Thank You, dear God,
that each meal is an opportunity to celebrate our love.**

When Our Cupboards Are Bare

Sometimes I feel overwhelmed at mealtime. I'm certain I simply don't have enough of the intangible ingredients I need to feed my family. Not enough time, not enough patience, not enough energy. And when I go to my refrigerator, looking for inspiration, I'm not surprised to find I don't have enough tangible ingredients either: I'm short on milk and bread; we're out of potatoes and onions, and the lettuce and broccoli are looking brown and yellow around their edges; only a sliver of butter is left on the dish, and just one lonely egg sits in solitary splendor in the egg holder. What am I going to do?

Times like these, I often feel like a failure as a mother. *After all*, whispers a little voice inside my head, *good mothers put warm, hearty meals on the table for their children.*

That's when I need to put all my little morsels of time and patience and energy into God's hands where they belong. He probably won't miraculously expand the pitiful contents of my larder—but when I give Him those intangible ingredients, I'm always surprised by the solutions I now have the strength to see. All God wants is for me to give Him what I have, no matter how impossibly small my offering may seem to me.

The rest is up to Him.

> *Our [families] are joyful and creative for me only when*
> *I can accept my own imperfections,*
> *when I can rush out with my sins of omission and commission*
> *and hang them on the cross as I hang out the laundry.*
> MADELINE L'ENGLE

CHICKEN ENCHILADAS

1 large onion, chopped
2 cloves garlic, finely chopped
1 tbsp vegetable oil
1 (4-oz) can diced green chiles
3 cups shredded cooked chicken

1 (10-oz) can mild enchilada sauce
2 cups shredded pepper-jack cheese
  (8 oz)
10 corn tortillas (6-inch)
1 cup half-and-half

Heat oven to 375°. Sauté onion and garlic in oil in medium-size skillet for 5 minutes. Add chiles, chicken, and sauce; cook 2 minutes. Stir in ½ cup cheese and remove from heat. Coat ovenproof 13x9x2-inch casserole with nonstick cooking spray. Wrap tortillas in damp paper towel; microwave 1 minute. Dip each tortilla in warm water, shaking off excess. Spoon ⅓ cup chicken mixture into each tortilla, roll up, and place seam side down in prepared pan. Top with half-and-half and sprinkle with remaining cheese. Bake for 10 minutes; then broil for 5 minutes until bubbly. Makes 5 servings.

At a dinner table,
when asked by his friend Emerson which dish he preferred,
Henry Thoreau replied nonchalantly, "The nearest."
HELEN NEARING

Remind us, Jesus, not to be fussy.

CHEESE AND MUSHROOM TART

1 prepared single-crust pie pastry, rolled out to 12 inches

Filling:

2 tbsp olive oil

2 cups thinly sliced onion
(about 1 large onion)

3 cups sliced white button mushrooms
(about 8 oz)

$\frac{1}{2}$ tsp dried thyme

$\frac{1}{2}$ tsp salt

$\frac{1}{2}$ tsp pepper

3 eggs

$\frac{1}{2}$ cup milk

$\frac{1}{8}$ tsp ground nutmeg

1 tbsp Dijon mustard

$1\frac{1}{2}$ cups shredded Monterey
Jack cheese (about 6 oz)

fresh thyme sprigs, for garnish

In 10-inch tart pan with removable bottom, place dough along bottom and up sides without stretching. Trim edges and prick bottom all over with fork. Line gently with foil. Fill foil with dried beans or pie weights. Bake crust in 400-degree oven for 5 minutes; cool on wire rack. To prepare filling: Heat oil in large nonstick skillet over medium heat and add onion, cooking about 10 minutes or until slightly softened. Add mushrooms, thyme, salt, and pepper; cook over high heat until vegetables are tender and liquid has evaporated (about 3 to 4 minutes). Mix eggs, milk, and nutmeg in large bowl; then combine with mushroom mixture. Brush mustard over bottom of pastry shell and sprinkle with cheese. Pour out mushroom mixture into shell. Bake in lower third of oven at 400° for 20 to 25 minutes until center is set and top is golden. Cool slightly on rack; garnish with thyme. Makes 12 servings.

Cooking can be an act of love and delight,
or it can be yet another exercise in racing through life on automatic pilot.
JANET LUHRS

Jesus, help each meal I prepare to be an expression of love.

BEEF TAMALE PIE

½ lb ground beef
2 cups shredded extra-sharp cheddar cheese (about 8 oz)
1 (8.5-oz) box corn-muffin mix
2 eggs
1 (12-oz) jar chunky salsa
1 tbsp chili powder
1 (7-oz) can whole kernel corn, drained (optional)

Heat oven to 450°. Coat 12x8x2-inch baking dish with nonstick cooking spray. In medium-size skillet, break up clumps of beef with wooden spoon and sauté 3 to 4 minutes or until no longer pink. Remove from heat. Mix 1 cup of the cheese with corn-muffin mix, eggs, salsa, chili powder, corn (if using), beef, and 2 cups water in large bowl until smooth. Pour into baking dish. Bake for 20 minutes. Sprinkle remaining 1 cup cheese over top and bake an additional 5 minutes, or until knife inserted in center comes out clean. Let stand 10 minutes. Makes 8 servings.

Each small task of everyday life is part of the total harmony of the universe.
THERESE OF LISIEUX

———

**Lord, help me to see that even the smallest
and most ordinary tasks are a part of Your kingdom.**

A Daily Celebration

Sometimes I tend to have a utilitarian approach to food: My family gets hungry so eventually I feed them. It's one of those never-ending and often thankless chores in my life, like doing the laundry or sweeping the kitchen floor. I forget that each meal can be a celebration, a time for enjoying one another and building memories.

> BEFORE WE EAT
> AT DINNER
> WE ALL JOIN HANDS
> AROUND THE TABLE,
> AND, FOR ME,
> THIS CIRCLE OF LOVE
> IS THE VISIBLE SYMBOL
> OF ALL I HOPE FOR.
> MADELINE L'ENGLE

One of the happy memories from my early childhood is of an ordinary meal. I'm sure my parents wouldn't even remember this particular supper. My brother and I were very small, and we began to get silly, taking two spoons each and putting them over our eyes. But instead of scolding us, my mother and father were relaxed enough that night to laugh with us, along with my older sisters. We were celebrating no special occasion, the food was our normal, everyday fare. But thirty-some years later, I still remember that meal—the shared laughter; the happiness of being together; the knowledge that we were loved.

CHICKEN-STUFFED PASTRIES

1 (4-oz) package light or
    regular creamy herbed cheese
1 tbsp low-fat (1%) milk
2 tsp bottled horseradish
1 tbsp unsalted butter
½ lb ground chicken
1 sheet (from a 17.25-oz package) puff pastry

1 apple (about 6 oz) peeled,
    cored, and diced
½ tsp salt
⅛ tsp pepper
½ cup chopped walnuts
½ tsp thyme

In bowl mixer, beat herbed cheese, milk, and horseradish until smooth. In large skillet, melt butter and cook chicken for 3 minutes. Add apple, salt, and pepper and cook until chicken is no longer pink (about 3 more minutes). Pour in cheese sauce, simmer until thickened, and remove from heat. In another clean, dry skillet, toast walnuts until lightly browned (about 7 minutes). Mix walnuts and thyme into filling. Heat oven to 425°. Unfold puff pastry to 10-inch square and cut into 3 strips along fold lines. Roll each piece into 12x4-inch rectangle and cut in half to create 6 rectangles. Spoon ⅓ cup filling in center of one side of each rectangle. Fold other half of pastry over filling and seal edges with a fork. Bake for 12 minutes or until golden. Makes 6 pastries.

And having food and raiment let us be therewith content.
1 TIMOTHY 6:8 KJV

**Remind us, God,
that You have blessed us with everything we truly need.**

CAULIFLOWER AND HAM CASSEROLE

1 tbsp chopped onion
3 tbsp butter or margarine, divided
2 tbsp all-purpose flour
½ tsp salt, optional
pepper to taste
1 cup milk
½ cup shredded cheddar cheese

1 medium head cauliflower,
  cut into florets, cooked
  and drained
2 cups cubed fully cooked ham
1 (4½-oz) jar sliced mushrooms, drained
1 (2-oz) jar diced pimientos, drained
6 saltine crackers, crumbled

In a saucepan over medium heat, sauté onion in 2 tablespoons of butter until tender. Stir in flour, salt if desired, and pepper. Gradually add milk; cook and stir for 2 minutes or until thick and bubbly. Remove from heat; stir in cheese until melted. Fold in cauliflower, ham, mushrooms, and pimientos. Pour into a greased 2-quart casserole. In a small saucepan, brown cracker crumbs in remaining butter; sprinkle over casserole. Cover and bake at 350° for 20 minutes. Uncover and bake 5–10 minutes longer or until heated through. Makes 6 servings.

Thou shalt feed my people. . . .
2 SAMUEL 5:2 KJV

Thank You, Lord, for the chance to feed Your people.

TARRAGON CHICKEN CASSEROLE

2 (10½-oz) cans condensed cream of chicken soup, undiluted
2 cups half-and-half
4 tsp dried tarragon
½ tsp pepper
1 (16-oz) package linguine or spaghetti, cooked and drained
6 cups cubed cooked chicken
½ cup grated Parmesan cheese
paprika, optional

In a large bowl, combine soup, cream, tarragon, and pepper. Stir in the linguine and chicken. Transfer to an ungreased 4-quart baking dish. Sprinkle with Parmesan cheese and paprika if desired. Bake, uncovered, at 350° for 30 minutes or until heated through. Yields 12 servings.

Save thy people, and bless thine inheritance:
feed them also, and lift them up forever.
PSALM 28:9 KJV

Lord, save us. . .bless us. . .feed us. . .
and lift us up above our sinful natures.

*And they continued stedfastly in the apostles' doctrine and fellowship
and in breaking of bread, and in prayers.*
ACTS 2:42

An Opportunity for Fellowship

The early church knew how important eating together was to their spiritual well-being. Notice in the verse above that breaking bread together seems to be as important as praying together—and the fellowship is stressed as much as the doctrine. As families, little "churches" living together within four walls, we, too, need to be "steadfast" about eating, fellowshipping, and praying together around the table. Not only does our physical well-being depend on these regular mealtimes, but our emotional and spiritual well-being does as well.

Always in every prayer of mine for you all making request with joy,

For your fellowship in the gospel. . .

Being confident of this very thing,

that he which hath begun a good work in you will perform it. . . .

PHILIPPIANS 1:4–6 KJV

PORK CHOPS AND SAUERKRAUT

3 cups sauerkraut, well drained
2 cups applesauce
½ cup chicken broth
½ lb sliced bacon, cooked
   and crumbled
1 tbsp brown sugar
1 tsp dried thyme

½ tsp ground mustard
½ tsp dried oregano
½ tsp salt
½ tsp pepper
6 pork chops (1-inch thick)
2 tbsp vegetable oil
½ tsp paprika

In a large bowl, combine the sauerkraut, applesauce, broth, bacon, brown sugar, and seasonings; spoon into an ungreased 13x9x2-inch baking dish. In a large skillet, brown pork chops in oil; drain. Place chops over the sauerkraut mixture. Sprinkle with paprika. Cover and bake at 350° for 1–1½ hours or until meat is tender and juices run clear. Makes 6 servings.

He shall feed his flock like a shepherd.
ISAIAH 40:11 KJV

**I'm glad, Lord Jesus, that You are my shepherd.
Thank You for taking such good care of us all.**

POOR MAN'S FILET MIGNON

2 lbs extra-lean ground beef
4 slices bread, crumbed
2 eggs, beaten
½ cup milk
2 tsp salt
1 tbsp minced onion

2 tsp dried celery flakes
½ tsp chili powder
1 (18-oz) bottle smoke-flavored
   barbecue sauce
12 slices uncooked bacon

Combine first 8 ingredients and 2 tablespoons barbecue sauce. Form into 12 thick patties. Wrap a bacon slice around the sides of each patty and secure with a toothpick. Bake on a rack at 350° for 50–60 minutes or until desired doneness. Baste frequently with remaining barbecue sauce the last 30 minutes. Makes 12 patties.

*They shall feed in the ways,
and their pastures shall be in all high places.
They shall not hunger. . . .*
ISAIAH 49:9–10 KJV

**God, I am so grateful that no matter where life leads me,
You always provide for me along the way.**

OLD-WORLD STUFFED PORK CHOPS

4 pork chops (½-inch thick)
1 to 2 tbsp cooking oil
salt and pepper to taste
3 cups dry, unseasoned bread cubes
1 (16-oz) can cream-style corn
1 egg, lightly beaten

1 tsp grated onion
½ tsp rubbed sage
½ tsp dried basil
½ tsp salt
½ tsp pepper

In a skillet, brown pork chops in oil on both sides; sprinkle with salt and pepper. Meanwhile, in a bowl, combine remaining ingredients and mix well. Alternate the pork chops and stuffing lengthwise in a greased 3-quart or 11x7x2-inch baking dish. Bake, uncovered, at 350° for 1 hour. Makes 4 servings.

I do like a bit of butter to my bread!

A.A. MILNE

**Jesus, thank You for giving us our daily bread—
and our daily butter, too!**

Surprise Gifts

One night last week my family sat in tense silence around the dinner table. My oldest daughter, who is deep in the throes of adolescence, had just announced that none of us understood her or truly loved her. I had snapped back at her, and now the others were afraid to say anything at all. We looked down at our plates while we ate and listened to the sound of each other chewing.

And then, with an angry stab of her fork, my daughter tried to take a bite of cherry tomato. As though magically possessing a life of its own, the tomato slipped out from under her fork and leapt into the air. It landed with a neat plop in my son's water glass.

For a moment, we all sat in silence, frozen. Then my husband snickered, and the two younger children began to giggle. I leaned my head on my hand and gave in to laughter, too. My oldest daughter scowled at us for a moment, but then her lips twitched, her eyes began to water, and at last she could no longer keep back her own giggles. We laughed until we forgot why we were laughing.

After supper, my daughter helped clear the table without being told. As she went past me on her way to the refrigerator, she leaned her head

> IF THERE BE THEREFORE ANY. . . COMFORT OF LOVE, IF ANY FELLOWSHIP OF THE SPIRIT. . . BE LIKEMINDED, HAVING THE SAME LOVE, BEING OF ONE ACCORD, OF ONE MIND. LET NOTHING BE DONE THROUGH STRIFE. . . .
>
> PHILIPPIANS 2:1–3 KJV

against me for just a moment. "I love you," I whispered in her ear. She only pushed her head harder against my shoulder, but I knew she heard me.

God sprinkles our lives with opportunities for love, lovely surprises He's hidden among the pots and pans, the forks and spoons, the hamburgers and cherry tomatoes of life. True fellowship doesn't necessarily mean we engage in spiritual discussions or have deep, intellectual conversations. No, real fellowship means we take advantage of all those unplanned opportunities. When we do, God's joy spills into our relationships with one another. He must like to hear us laugh.

A meal is meant to be a "mini-vacation."
A meal is meant to be seen and understood and experienced
as a "mini-time to let your hair down and be your true self."
A meal is meant to be an event that gives us the human
experience of being our true selves in joy.
A meal is meant to re-create us.

ROBERT FABING

CRAB-STUFFED POTATOES

4 medium baking potatoes
½ cup butter or margarine
⅓ to ½ cup light cream
1 tsp salt
½ tsp pepper
½ cup finely chopped green
  onions or chives

1 cup (4 oz) shredded cheddar cheese
1 (6½-oz) can crabmeat, drained,
  flaked, and cartilage removed or
  1 (8-oz) package imitation
  crabmeat, cut up
paprika

Bake potatoes at 425° for 45–55 minutes or until tender. When cool enough to handle, cut potatoes in half lengthwise. Carefully scoop out pulp into a bowl, leaving a thin shell. Set shells aside. Beat or mash potato pulp with butter, cream, salt, and pepper until smooth. Using a fork, stir in onions or chives and cheese. Gently mix in crab. Stuff shells and sprinkle with paprika. Return to oven for 15 minutes or until heated through. Makes 8 servings.

They shall feed every one in his place.
JEREMIAH 6:3 KJV

**Thank You, Lord,
that You have a place for each of us in Your kingdom.**

SWISS STEAK

½ cup all-purpose flour
1 tsp salt
½ tsp pepper
1½ to 2 lbs beef round steak,
   trimmed
2 tbsp cooking oil

1 cup chopped celery
1 cup chopped onion
½ lb fresh mushrooms, sliced
1 cup water
1 garlic clove, minced
1 tbsp steak sauce

Combine flour, salt, and pepper. Cut steak into serving-size pieces; dredge in flour mixture. In a skillet, brown steak in oil. Drain and place in a 2½-qt. casserole. Top with celery, onion, and mushrooms. Combine water, garlic, and steak sauce; pour over vegetables. Cover and bake at 350° for 1½ hours or until meat is tender. Makes 6 servings.

But I will bring Israel back to his own pasture and. . .
his appetite will be satisfied.
JEREMIAH 50:19

God, I know You don't want Your children to go hungry.
Thank You for meeting my family's needs.

Pork Chops Olé

6 loin pork chops (½-inch thick)
2 tbsp cooking oil
seasoned salt and pepper to taste
½ cup uncooked long grain rice
1½ cups water

1 (8-oz) can tomato sauce
½ envelope taco seasoning mix
  (2 tbsp)
1 medium green pepper, chopped
½ cup shredded cheddar cheese

In a large skillet, brown pork chops in oil; sprinkle with seasoned salt and pepper. Meanwhile, in a greased 13x9x2-inch baking dish, combine rice, water, tomato sauce, and taco seasoning; mix well. Arrange chops over rice; top with green pepper. Cover and bake at 350° for 1½ hours. Uncover and sprinkle with cheese; return to oven until cheese is melted. Makes 4–6 servings.

*And I will set up one shepherd over them, and he shall feed them. . .
he shall feed them, and he shall be their shepherd.*
EZEKIEL 34:23 KJV

**Sometimes, Lord,
You know I go running off to other "shepherds,"
expecting them to feed me.
Remind me that You alone are my Shepherd—
and You alone can nourish my heart, my soul, and my body.**

Nightly Communion

As mothers forced to furiously juggle not only our own busy schedules but also the separate schedules of each member of our families, sometimes eating meals together seems an impossible ideal. In my own family, we try to keep our afternoon and evening commitments to a minimum, hoping to simplify our lives so that we can depend on coming together around the supper table each night. But sometimes, despite our best efforts, it just doesn't happen. One member of my family has a sports event, another has a Scouts meeting; my husband has an after-hours appointment, while I have a church function I'm committed to attending. We all scramble to grab a quick meal on the run between our various commitments.

Yes, some nights just work out that way. But *every* night doesn't have to be like that. If your family makes a weekly schedule for meals and menus, make sure you look ahead to outside commitments that may conflict with mealtimes. With a little foresight, some appointments can be rescheduled. After consideration, we may decide some aren't that important after all and can be dispensed with altogether. Other times, splitting the family into smaller pieces can even build our closeness. For instance, on lacrosse nights, my husband and youngest daughter go to my son's game together; the littlest member of the family enjoys the chance to have Daddy to herself during the game, while my oldest daughter and I have an opportunity to be alone together and catch up on "woman talk."

The important thing is to make sure that meals are times of closeness and communication. Christ Himself told us clearly just how important a shared meal can be. After all, He chose an ordinary supper to be the symbol of our fellowship with His life and death.

*Then at the proper time
Jesus and the twelve apostles
sat down together at the table.
Jesus said, "I have looked forward
to this hour with deep longing,
anxious to eat this Passover meal
with you. . . ."*

LUKE 22:14–15 NLT

BAVARIAN SAUSAGE SUPPER

2 cups coleslaw mix
1 cup thinly sliced carrots
2 tbsp butter or margarine
2½ cups water
½ lb fully cooked kielbasa or Polish sausage, sliced
1 (4½-oz) package quick-cooking noodles and
    sour cream chive sauce mix
½ tsp caraway seeds (optional)

In a large skillet, sauté coleslaw mix and carrots in butter until crisp-tender. Add water and bring to a boil. Stir in remaining ingredients. Return to a boil; cook for 8 minutes or until noodles are tender, stirring occasionally. Makes 5 servings.

Now the LORD will feed them as a lamb in a large place.
HOSEA 4:16 KJV

**Sometimes, Jesus,
I feel surrounded by frustration and limitations.
Help me find that large, open space
where You seek to feed my soul.**

MEATBALL SUB CASSEROLE

⅓ cup chopped green onions
½ cup seasoned bread crumbs
3 tbsp grated Parmesan cheese
1 lb ground beef
1 loaf (1 lb) Italian bread,
    cut into 1-inch slices
1 (8-oz) package cream cheese,
    softened

½ cup mayonnaise
1 tsp Italian seasoning
½ tsp pepper
2 cups (8 oz) shredded
    mozzarella cheese
1 (28-oz) jar spaghetti sauce
1 cup water
2 garlic cloves, minced

In a bowl, combine onions, crumbs, and Parmesan cheese. Add beef and mix well. Shape into 1-inch balls; place on a rack in a shallow baking pan. Bake at 400° for 15–20 minutes or until no longer pink. Meanwhile, arrange bread in a single layer in an ungreased 13x9x2-inch baking dish. (All of the bread might not be used.) Combine cream cheese, mayonnaise, Italian seasoning, and pepper; spread over the bread. Sprinkle with ½ cup mozzarella. Combine sauce, water, and garlic; add meatballs. Pour over cheese mixture; sprinkle with remaining mozzarella. Bake, uncovered, at 350° for 30 minutes or until heated through. Makes 6–8 servings.

And he shall stand and feed in the strength of the LORD.
MICAH 5:4 KJV

**Some days, Lord, You know my faith is pretty wobbly.
Remind me then to feed on Your strength.**

HAM AND CHEESE POTATO BAKE

1 (24-oz) package frozen O'Brien hash brown potatoes
2 cups cubed fully cooked ham
$\frac{1}{2}$ cup shredded cheddar cheese, divided
1 small onion, chopped
2 cups (16 oz) sour cream
1 (10$\frac{1}{2}$-oz) can condensed cheddar cheese soup, undiluted
1 (10$\frac{1}{2}$-oz) can condensed cream of potato soup, undiluted
$\frac{1}{2}$ tsp pepper

In a large bowl, combine potatoes, ham, $\frac{1}{2}$ cup cheese, and onion. In another bowl, combine sour cream, soups, and pepper; add to potato mixture and mix well. Transfer to a greased 3-quart baking dish. Sprinkle with remaining cheese. Bake, uncovered, at 350° for 60–65 minutes or until bubbly and potatoes are tender. Let stand for 10 minutes before serving. Makes 10–12 servings.

They will eat and lie down and no one will make them afraid.
ZEPHANIAH 3:13

**O God, I'm so glad that because of Jesus,
we can eat and rest and never be afraid.**

A Chance to Practice Love

As a mother, I have to confess that sometimes as I listen to my family snipe at each other around the supper table, I wonder why so many experts tell us that eating together is important to a family's health. On school nights, we all tend to be tired and crabby by the time we sit down to eat; at least one child is sure to be unhappy with the evening's menu; my husband or I snap when the milk gets spilled; and if there's dessert, somehow one child always ends up with a piece that's fractionally smaller than the others'. Some nights I can't help but think how much more peaceful it would be if we fed the children first, the way they do in old-fashioned books about wealthy English people. That way my husband and I could have a little uninterrupted quiet conversation.

But when I read the Gospels, I get the impression that even Jesus' meals weren't always calm and spiritual. From the sounds of things, He, too, had to listen to some squabbling around the table. But that didn't keep Him from sitting down to eat again and again with both His friends and His enemies. He could have withdrawn Himself at mealtime; He could have said He needed some time alone for peace and quiet. But He didn't. He knew that every time we draw together, even for the brief space of a meal, we have the chance to show each other our love.

Yes, as a family maybe it would be easier if we all went our separate ways. Then we wouldn't have to deal with all the conflicts that are a part of normal family life. But learning to work out our petty disagreements is an important lesson in being a part of Christ's body here on earth. Love isn't so much an emotion as it is a way of living—and like any skill, it comes easier each time we put it into practice.

55

That's why family meals are so important; because each and every time we sit down together around the table we have one more opportunity to put our love for each other into practice.

No, it's not easy. But it is worth the effort.

A meal is an experience not only of biological food but also of emotional, physiological, intellectual, and spiritual food: sustenance. "Human beings do not live by bread alone" (Matthew 4:4), says the Lord. . . . A meal is an event for the soul of a person as well as for the body.

ROBERT FABING

PIZZA POTATO CASSEROLE

1 lb ground beef
1 medium green pepper, chopped
1 medium onion, chopped
1 (11⅛-oz) can condensed Italian tomato soup, undiluted
1 (4½-oz) jar sliced mushrooms, drained
2 cups (8 oz) shredded mozzarella cheese
1 (32-oz) package frozen "hash browns" or potato balls

In a skillet, cook the beef, pepper and onion until meat is no longer pink; drain. Add soup and mushrooms. Transfer to a greased 13x9x2-inch baking dish. Top with cheese and potatoes. Bake uncovered at 400° for 30–35 minutes or until golden brown. Makes 6–8 servings.

For the Lamb which is in the midst of the throne shall feed them.
REVELATION 7:17 KJV

**What an amazing thought!
The Lamb, the King of all creation,
nourishes our family.**

FISH STICK SUPPER

1 (12-oz) package frozen, shredded hash brown potatoes, thawed
4 eggs
2 cups milk
1 tbsp dried minced onion
1 tbsp snipped fresh dill or 1 tsp dill weed
1½ tsp seasoned salt
⅛ tsp pepper
1 cup (4 oz) shredded cheddar cheese
1 (12-oz) package frozen fish sticks (about 18)

Break apart hash browns with fork; set aside. In a large bowl, beat eggs and milk. Add onion, dill, seasoned salt, and pepper. Stir in hash browns and cheese. Transfer to a greased 11x7x2-inch baking dish and arrange fish sticks over top. Bake, uncovered, at 350° for 50 minutes or until top is golden brown and fish flakes with a fork. Let stand for 5 minutes before cutting. Makes 6 servings.

Feed the flock of God which is among you.
1 PETER 5:2 KJV

**Thank You, Lord,
for the little "flock" I have the privilege to feed.**

CHICKEN PARMIGIANA

4 boneless, skinless chicken breast
   halves
1 (6-oz) can tomato paste
$\frac{1}{2}$ cup water
2 garlic gloves, minced
1 tbsp dried parsley flakes
1 tsp salt
$\frac{1}{2}$ tsp pepper

$\frac{1}{2}$ tsp Italian seasoning
$\frac{1}{2}$ tsp dried oregano
$\frac{1}{2}$ tsp crushed red pepper flakes
   (optional)
2 cups (8 oz) shredded
   mozzarella cheese
$\frac{1}{2}$ cup grated Parmesan cheese

Layer chicken in a greased 8-inch square baking pan. Combine tomato paste, water, garlic, and seasonings in a saucepan and bring to a boil. Pour over chicken and bake uncovered at 400° for 15–20 minutes or until chicken juices run clear. Sprinkle with cheese and bake an additional 10 minutes or until cheese is melted. Makes 4 servings.

Then shalt thou delight thyself in the LORD;
and I will cause thee to ride upon the high places of the earth, and feed thee. . . .
ISAIAH 58:14 KJV

**Even on the busiest, most hectic days,
Jesus, help me to delight myself in You.**

Because we cannot see Christ, we cannot express our love to Him in person.
But our [child] we can see, and we can do for him or her
what we would love to do for Jesus if He were visible.
MOTHER TERESA

The Silent Listener

When I was growing up, my mother used to have a little plaque that read, "Jesus is the unseen guest at every meal, the silent listener to every conversation." The words always gave me goose bumps. They reminded me that at every meal, Jesus was sitting close beside me, enjoying the food and conversation, keeping me company, loving me. Even though I couldn't see Him, His presence was real.

Today as I set the table for my family's supper, I still like to think of that unseen Guest. Cooking supper for my family—even when the task seems tedious and less than rewarding—is a chance to serve my Lord. I try to make sure I make Him welcome at our table. And I remind myself that as I interact with my children and husband, Jesus hears my conversation. I'm more apt to speak words of love when I remember He is listening.

We ought not to be weary of doing little things for the love of God,
who regards not the greatness of the work,
but the love with which it is performed.
BROTHER LAWERENCE

*To see God in
work, cooking, prayer, community. . .
is to enter into the mystery of
the incarnation.*

BRIAN C. TAYLOR

BROCCOLI HAM STROGANOFF

2 cups frozen chopped broccoli
1 tbsp water
1 tbsp butter or margarine
½ cup chopped onion
3 tbsp all-purpose flour
Hot cooked noodles

1 (10½-oz) can chicken broth
2 cups cubed fully cooked ham
1 (8-oz) cup sour cream
1 (4½-oz) jar sliced mushrooms,
    drained

Place broccoli and water in a 1-quart microwave-safe bowl. Cover and microwave on high for 3–5 minutes or until the broccoli is tender, stirring once. Drain; set aside and keep warm. In another microwave-safe bowl, heat butter, uncovered, on high for 20 seconds or until melted. Add onion; cover and microwave on high for 2 minutes or until tender. Stir in flour until blended. Gradually stir in broth; mix well. Microwave uncovered on high for 4–6 minutes or until thickened and bubbly, stirring once. Add the ham, sour cream, mushrooms, and reserved broccoli; mix well. Cook uncovered on high for 3–5 minutes or until heated through, stirring once. Serve over noodles. Makes 4 servings. Serve with fresh tomato wedges.

I will feed them in a good pasture. . .and in a fat pasture shall they feed. . . .
 EZEKIEL 34:14 KJV

***Thank You, Jesus, that we don't have to have "skinny hearts."
Instead, You want us to be well fed with Your love.***

GROUND BEEF AND BISCUITS

1½ lbs ground beef
½ cup chopped celery
½ cup chopped onion
2 tbsp all-purpose flour
1 tsp salt
½ tsp dried oregano

⅛ tsp pepper
2 (8-oz) cans tomato sauce
1 (10-oz) package frozen peas
1 (7½-oz) tube refrigerated
  buttermilk biscuits
1 cup (4 oz) shredded
  cheddar cheese

Cook beef, celery, and onion in a skillet over medium heat until meat is no longer pink, and celery is tender; drain. Add flour, salt, oregano, and pepper; blend well. Add tomato sauce and peas; simmer for 5 minutes. Transfer to a greased 13x9x2-inch baking dish. Separate biscuits and arrange over beef mixture. Sprinkle with cheese. Bake uncovered at 350° for 20 minutes or until biscuits are golden and cheese is melted. Makes 6 servings.

I will feed my flock, and I will cause them to lie down, saith the Lord GOD.
EZEKIEL 34:15 KJV

**Help me to trust You, Lord God,
for all the rest and nourishment I need.**

Getting Dinner in the Morning:

Slow Cooker Recipes

True dining is an experience available to us all. . . .
It requires only a desire. . .to please,
to share the best that life has to offer.
It claims only a little time, a dabble of creativity. . .
lots of love, and like magic, the scene is set for wonder!

LEO BUSCAGLIA

Be joyful at your Feast. . . .

DEUTERONOMY 16:14

When it comes to cooking, there really isn't a right or wrong way of doing things. What worked for your mother and mother-in-law may not work for you. What works for you may not work for me—and vice versa. I have an office in my home where I work full time, so my routines will be different from those of a mother who works outside her home—and both will be different from those of a mother who is busy with a houseful of preschoolers.

Each of our schedules is different. As mothers who are all busy juggling our lives, we need to remember that juggling is not a competition sport. God does not compare us to each other, and we are each uniquely and infinitely loved. Besides, the juggler who spends her energy worrying about the success of the person juggling beside her will be more apt to lose her own rhythm!

But we can learn from each other's successes. Getting dinner in the morning is something I've found *does* work for me. I'm usually in the kitchen anyway while the kids eat their breakfast and get ready for school, and I'm less stressed than I am later in the day. I throw a bunch of ingredients in the crock pot—and then I have the pleasure of smelling it cook all day. Even if the end of my workday is tense and frantic, I have the comforting knowledge that supper will be ready (or nearly ready) whenever we want it.

The recipes that follow are all designed for slow cookers. If you have time in your morning, you can start these meals then, before your workday, and then go about your business for the rest of the day until evening, when you'll find your dinner waiting for its finishing touches. Most of these slow cooker meals can also be reheated on the stove another day.

JUGGLING TIP:
If once a week you sit down and
make your menus for the seven days ahead,
you may want to have a calendar where you
keep track of both menus and activities.
That way you can match preparation times to your schedule.
A large calendar posted on your refrigerator
works well as a place to jot down the week's meals
along with each family member's events.
Or you could keep it all in your Daytimer.

DILL TURKEY CHOWDER

1 lb uncooked turkey breast slices,
  cut into 1-inch pieces
½ tsp garlic pepper
½ tsp salt
6 to 8 new potatoes,
  cut into 1-inch pieces
1 medium onion, chopped (½ cup)

2 medium carrots, sliced (1 cup)
2 tsp dried dill weed
2½ cups chicken broth
1 (15½-oz) can whole
  kernel corn, drained
1 cup half-and-half
3 tbsp cornstarch

Put turkey in a 4- to 5-quart slow cooker and sprinkle with garlic pepper and salt. Stir in next 6 ingredients. Cover and cook on low heat for 6 to 8 hours or until vegetables are tender. Combine half-and-half and cornstarch; add to chowder gradually until well blended. Cover and cook on high heat about 20 minutes, stirring occasionally, until thickened. Makes 6 servings. Serve with French bread slices and a large, crisp green salad tossed with your favorite vinaigrette.

*I can accept that some of my creations will not work
and some will, and so what? . . .
I can think about who will eat this meal I am cooking
and who will receive the love that I put into it.*

JANET LUHRS

Lord, help me remember to put some love into each meal I cook.

TURKEY & VEGETABLES WITH CORNMEAL DUMPLINGS

2 turkey thighs (about 2 lbs), skin
  and bones removed
1 (15½-oz) can whole kernel corn,
  undrained
1 (8-oz) can tomato sauce
2 tbsp all-purpose flour
1 tsp chili powder

1 tsp salt
½ tsp pepper
Cornmeal Dumplings
  (recipe on page 71)
1 medium zucchini, sliced
  (2 cups)
½ tsp salt

Place turkey in slow cooker. Combine corn, tomato sauce, flour, chili powder, salt, and pepper; pour over turkey. Cover and cook on low for 8 to 10 hours or until turkey is no longer pink when cut in the center. Drop prepared cornmeal dumplings by spoonfuls onto hot turkey mixture. Arrange zucchini slices around dumplings and sprinkle with ½ tsp salt. Cover and cook on high for 35 to 45 minutes or until toothpick inserted in dumplings comes out clean. Makes 6 servings.

CORNMEAL DUMPLINGS

½ cup all-purpose flour
½ cup yellow cornmeal
½ cup milk
2 tbsp vegetable oil
1 tsp baking powder

½ tsp salt
½ tsp ground thyme leaves
1 egg
1 small onion, finely chopped
  (½ cup)

Mix all ingredients. Sprinkle dumplings with about 4 slices of crumbled bacon before serving to add a smoky flavor.

A meal is a social event.
It is a human experience that nourishes our human needs for
intimacy, emotionally and psychologically,
as well as nourishing our physical bodies with food.
ROBERT FABING

Jesus, make our mealtimes truly nourishing—
emotionally and spiritually, as well as physically.

Unconditional Love

I have enough of my mother in me that I find satisfaction in throwing together a meal that's both nourishing and tasty. But having said that, notice my choice of words: "I find satisfaction in *throwing together* a meal." My mother, on the other hand, plans all her meals with tender and painstaking care.

As guilty as I sometimes feel about this sad truth, I simply don't find my greatest daily pleasure in preparing my family's meals. Instead, I find my most consistent delight in writing rather than cooking, and meal preparation more often than not seems like an inconvenient interruption in my day. I have other things I'd rather be doing.

But why do we all feel we have to live up to someone else's standards? If you feel creative and satisfied when you're cooking, then by all means, make time in your life for this wonderful talent you've been given. But if, like me, your gifts lie in other areas, then why not give yourself permission to be the woman God created you to be (instead of trying to be someone you're not)?

God doesn't expect us to do every single thing perfectly. And being a member of His kingdom is not a contest, nor do we have to meet a quality requirement before He lets us in. Jesus Christ is the Door into the Kingdom of Heaven. Through Him—and through no effort of our own—we are accepted and loved and valued.

In the end, the most important thing about any meal is whether Christ is present with us as we eat it. Even peanut butter sandwiches can be a feast when we acknowledge His presence with our family—and He's delighted to join even our simplest meals.

He's not fussy.

MEDITERRANEAN POT ROAST

3-lb beef boneless chuck roast
1 tsp salt
1 tbsp dried Italian seasoning
1 large clove garlic, finely chopped
$\frac{1}{3}$ cup oil-packed sun-dried tomatoes, drained and chopped
$\frac{1}{2}$ cup sliced pitted Kalamata or ripe olives
$\frac{1}{2}$ cup beef broth
$\frac{1}{2}$ cup frozen pearl onions (from 16-oz bag)

Coat 12-inch skillet with cooking spray; heat over medium-high heat. Brown beef in skillet about 5 minutes, turning once. Sprinkle with salt, Italian seasoning, and garlic; remove from skillet. With seasoned side up, place beef in slow cooker. Layer tomatoes and olives over roast. Add broth and onions. Cover and cook on low heat for 5 to 6 hours or until beef is tender. Remove beef from slow cooker; cover and allow to stand for 15 minutes. Slice and serve with beef juice and onions. Fluffy homemade mashed potatoes are the perfect complement for beef roast. Makes 8 to 10 servings.

Behold the fowls of the air. . .your heavenly Father feedeth them.
MATTHEW 6:26 KJV

Each time I look out my kitchen window and see a bird fly past, remind me, Lord, that You're providing not only for that bird but for my family as well.

Cajun Beef Stew

½ cup Caribbean jerk marinade
1½ lbs beef stew meat
4 medium red potatoes (about 12 oz), cut into fourths
⅓ cup all-purpose flour
1 tbsp spicy Cajun seasoning
1 (14½-oz) can diced tomatoes, undrained
3 cups frozen stir-fry bell peppers and onions (from 16-oz bag)

Place beef in a glass or plastic dish and pour marinade over top; coat completely with marinade and allow to stand for 15 minutes. Spray inside of slow cooker with cooking spray. Put potatoes in slow cooker. Combine flour and Cajun seasoning; toss with beef and marinade, coating well. Pour out beef and marinade on potatoes. Add tomatoes. Cover and cook on low for 7 to 8 hours until beef is tender. Stir in vegetables; cover and cook on low for an additional 15 to 30 minutes, or until vegetables are tender. Makes 4 to 6 servings. Also tastes delicious served over rice.

*"The bread of this world" is all that nourishes and energizes us,
not only food but the love of friends and family.*
KATHLEEN NORRIS

Thank You, God, for all the many forms of "bread" You give me.

VEGETABLE BEEF BARLEY SOUP

½ cup frozen green beans
⅔ cup frozen whole kernel corn
1½ lbs beef stew meat
½ cup chopped bell pepper
1 large onion, chopped (1 cup)
⅔ cup uncooked barley
1½ cups water
1 tsp salt

1 tsp chopped fresh or
  ½ tsp dried thyme leaves
½ tsp pepper
2 (14½-oz) cans ready-to-
  serve beef broth
2 (14½-oz) cans diced tomatoes
  with roasted garlic, undrained
1 (8-oz) can tomato sauce

Partially thaw and separate green beans and corn by rinsing with cold water. Mix with remaining ingredients in slow cooker. Cover and cook on low for 8 to 9 hours or until vegetables and barley are tender. Makes 10 servings. Serve with a sprinkling of Parmesan cheese and herb-flavored croutons.

Thus saith the LORD God of Israel, Let my people go,
that they may hold a feast unto me in the wilderness.

EXODUS 5:1 KJV

———————

**Free us, God, from the captivity of sin and selfishness,
so that we may feast on You.**

SPANISH CHICKEN

1 large onion, chopped (1 cup)
2 cloves garlic, finely chopped
1 large red bell pepper, chopped
   (1½ cups)
1 tsp dried oregano leaves
½ to 1 tsp crushed red pepper
1 lb turkey Italian sausages,
   cut into 1-inch pieces
3 cups hot cooked rice

1½ lbs boneless, skinless chicken
   breast halves, cut into 1-inch pieces
1 (28-oz) can diced tomatoes,
   undrained
1 (6-oz) can tomato paste
1 (14-oz) can artichoke heart quarters,
   drained
1 (4-oz) can sliced ripe olives, drained

Spray inside of slow cooker with cooking spray. With the exception of artichoke hearts, olives, and rice, mix all ingredients in slow cooker. Cover and cook on low for 6 to 8 hours, or until sausages and chicken are no longer pink. Add artichoke hearts and olives; heat through. Serve with cooked rice. Makes 6 servings.

And this day shall be unto you for a memorial;
and ye shall keep it a feast to the LORD. . . .
EXODUS 12:14 KJV

**Lord, may my children have happy memories of mealtimes.
May each of our meals, no matter how ordinary,
be a feast to You.**

A Special Guest

Tamar lay on her bed and stared up at the ceiling in frustration. Why did she have to be sick today, of all days, when the Master was coming to her house to eat? Ever since she got up this morning, she had tried to ignore the fever that made her eyes blur and her skin hurt, but now she had collapsed while she was kneading the bread. Her daughter ran to help her, and as soon as she touched her, she cried out, "Mother, you have a fever!" With her husband Peter's help, they had carried Tamar to her bed.

Tamar ground her teeth. She had wanted so much to cook a meal for Jesus. It was the one thing she was really good at, the one thing she knew she did better than anyone else. Tonight's meal would have been her love offering to Him.

As her fever climbed still higher, her mind wandered over the past weeks. She had seen Jesus do so many miracles of love. He always had a smile, a touch for everyone, no matter how insignificant the person was, no matter how small or dirty or sick. His love simply reached out with open arms to everyone.

Watching Him, Tamar had found herself looking at her own life for the first time. She had always done what was expected of her, her whole life, without giving it much thought. As a young girl she had obeyed her parents; when she had married, she had been a good and dutiful wife; when her children were born, she gave herself to their care; and now that she was a widow, she cooked the meals and helped with the cleaning in the household of her daughter and her husband Peter. It was an ordinary life, but she knew she was blessed to have always had food and a roof, when so many women, especially widows, had so little. Now and then, especially as she grew older, she was a little tired of all the work, all the endless bread that had to be baked, the fruit that had to be cleaned, the meat that had to be stewed or dried and salted.

For the most part, though, she simply didn't think about it one way or the other. That wasn't her way—until knowing Jesus had made her stop and think. What did it all mean? The question began to haunt her. All the work and endless meals she had prepared, did it all count for anything?

But as she watched Jesus day after day and listened to His words, she began to think she saw the answer in His eyes. There was nothing too small to interest Him; in the light of His love *everything* mattered. The details of the most ordinary lives were precious in His sight.

When she had realized that, something in her heart began to change. She wasn't like some of the younger women who seemed to feel so free to spill out their hearts to Jesus. No, that had never been her way, either. She was a quiet woman, a woman who spoke little because she was too busy to take the time, a practical woman who had never expressed her heart much to anyone.

But she knew how to cook. After preparing meals all these years, she ought to. As a mother and a wife, she knew how to feed a man—and she longed to give Jesus a meal.

Tonight had been the opportunity she had waited for. And now here she was sick in her bed. She was never sick; she didn't have time to be sick. How could her body have let her down like this? How could she please the Master when she was too weak to even lift her head off the pillow?

The sound of voices in the other room told her their guests had arrived. She turned her head toward the wall, and angry tears leaked out beneath her lids.

"Mother?" Her daughter's soft voice made her open her eyes and turn her head toward the doorway. "The Master is here. He wants to see you."

"No." Tamar moved her head weakly back and forth. "I don't want Him to see me like this." She shut her eyes, as though she could hide herself behind her eyelids.

Someone touched her hand. With a sigh, she opened her eyes and looked up into Jesus' face. "Master," she whispered. "I'm so sorry. I wanted. . .I wanted to cook for You."

He smiled, then knelt on the floor beside her bed. "Tamar," He asked gently, "do you love Me?"

Her eyes filled once more with tears. "Yes, Lord. I do."

"Then I am just as pleased with you now, when you are flat on your back, too weak to stand, as when you bustle around your kitchen. Even sick in bed, you can serve Me."

"But how, Jesus?" Her head hurt too much for her to make sense of His words.

"Whatever you are doing, give Me your heart. Offer even your sickness to Me. That is all the service I require." His hand touched her hot forehead. "I care little about the success or failure of your efforts. All I want is for you to do each thing, no matter how small, with your whole heart, as an offering to Me. Will you do that for Me, Tamar?"

Tamar struggled with her frustration. After all, cooking was something she could do well. . . How could her sickness serve Jesus? But if that's what He wanted. . . With a deep sigh, she felt her body relax against the mat. "If that's what You want, Lord. . .then I will be sick. . .for You."

His smile told her she had pleased Him. She realized her terrible headache was gone, and she lifted her head. To her surprise, her muscles felt steady and strong, filled with a new energy, and she sat up in bed. "But, Lord," she said after a moment, "I feel as though I might be able to get up after all!"

His smile grew wider as He got to His feet and helped her stand. She looked up at Him shyly. "Would you mind if I cooked You that meal after all, Lord?"

"So long as you do it with your whole heart, Tamar. Remember—that's the only service I require."

CHICKEN NOODLE SOUP

½ lb boneless, skinless chicken thighs, cut into 1-inch pieces

2 medium stalks celery (with leaves), sliced (1½ cups)

1 large carrot, chopped (½ cup)

1 medium onion, chopped (½ cup)

1 (14½-oz) can diced tomatoes, undrained

1 (14½-oz) can ready-to-serve chicken broth

1 tsp dried thyme leaves

1 (10-oz) package frozen green peas

1 cup frozen home-style egg noodles (from 12-oz package)

Spray 10-inch skillet with cooking spray and heat over medium heat. Brown chicken in skillet for 5 minutes, stirring frequently. Mix chicken and next 6 ingredients in slow cooker. Cook, covered, on low heat for 6½ to 7 hours or until chicken is no longer pink in center. Add peas and noodles and cook an additional 10 minutes or until noodles are tender. Makes 6 servings. Stir in 1 tablespoon chopped fresh parsley just before serving.

Weekday cooks [need] a kitchen artistry of a different sort.
It calls for Grandma's nearly lost art of simple, solid cooking.
It calls for thrift and organization as well as flexibility, good nutrition, and ease.
It calls for knowing how to rummage in the pantry and forage through the refrigerator.

MICHELE URVATER

God, while I rummage in the pantry and forage through the refrigerator, keep my heart fixed on You.

PORK CHOPS WITH APPLE CHERRY STUFFING

1 (6-oz) package herb stuffing mix
2 medium stalks celery, chopped (1 cup)
1 medium tart cooking apple, peeled and chopped
1 medium onion, chopped (½ cup)
1 cup dried cherries
½ cup margarine or butter, melted
1 cup chicken broth
6 pork boneless loin chops (about ½-inch thick)

Coat inside of slow cooker with cooking spray. Combine all ingredients except pork. Spoon half of stuffing mixture into slow cooker; top with pork. Spread remaining stuffing over pork. Cover and cook on low heat for 6 to 8 hours or until pork is tender. Makes 6 servings. Steamed green beans and baked potatoes are a tasty side dish for the pork chops.

To morrow is a feast to the LORD.
EXODUS 32:5 KJV

**Thank You, Lord, that every day brings us
opportunities to feast on Your name.**

EASY CHOP SUEY

1 lb ground pork or beef
1 medium onion, chopped
   (1/2 cup)
1 medium stalk celery, coarsely chopped
   (1/2 cup)
1/2 tsp pepper
1/2 cup soy sauce
1/3 cup uncooked regular long-grain rice

1 (10 1/2-oz) can condensed
   cream of mushroom soup
1 cup water
3 cups frozen stir-fry vegetables
   (from 16-oz bag)
Crisp chow mein noodles,
   if desired

Spray inside of slow cooker with cooking spray. Cook pork or beef over medium-high heat for 5 minutes, stirring occasionally. Add onion and celery and cook an additional 5 minutes or until meat is brown; drain. Stir in next 5 ingredients and pour into slow cooker. Cover and cook on low for 8 to 9 hours. Add vegetables; cover and cook over low heat for 15 more minutes, or until vegetables are tender. Serve with noodles. Makes 4 to 6 servings.

*Each day brings with it not only the necessity of eating
but the renewal of our love of and in God.*

KATHLEEN NORRIS

**May I use each mealtime as a chance to turn
my heart toward You, Lord.**

Lord of all pots and pans and things,
Since I've no time to be
A saint by doing lovely things, or
Watching late with Thee,
Or dreaming in the dawn light, or
Storming heaven's gates,
Make me a saint by getting meals and
Washing up the plates.

Warm all the kitchen with Thy love, and
Light it with Thy peace.
Forgive me all my worryings, and make
All grumbling cease.
Thou who didst love to give men food
In room or by the sea,
Accept this service that I do,
I do it unto Thee.

CECILY HALLECK

WINTER VEGETABLE STEW

1 (28-oz) can plum tomatoes
4 medium red potatoes, cut into
  ½-inch pieces
4 medium stalks celery, cut into ½-inch
  pieces (2 cups)
3 medium carrots, cut into ½-inch pieces
  (1½ cups)
2 medium parsnips, peeled and cut into
  ½-inch pieces

2 medium leeks, cut into ½-inch
  pieces
1 (14½-oz) can ready-to-serve
  chicken broth
½ tsp dried thyme leaves
½ tsp dried rosemary leaves
½ tsp salt
3 tbsp cornstarch
3 tbsp cold water

Drain tomatoes and reserve liquid. Chop tomatoes. In slow cooker, combine tomatoes, liquid, and all ingredients except cornstarch and water; cover and cook 8 to 10 hours on low heat, or until vegetables are tender. Mix cornstarch and water; gradually stir into slow cooker until blended. Cover and cook another 20 minutes on high heat setting until thickened, stirring occasionally. Sprinkle chopped fresh chives or thyme leaves and shredded Parmesan cheese over top. Serve with a loaf of crusty Italian bread. Serves 8.

Joy and gladness, and cheerful feasts; therefore love the truth and peace.
ZECHARIAH 8:19 KJV

Jesus, by Your grace, make each meal we eat together a cheerful feast, filled with joy and gladness. Fill our family with truth and peace.

PORK CHOP DINNER

4 lean pork boneless loin chops, about ½-inch thick
2 medium onions, sliced
1 (4½-oz) jar sliced mushrooms, drained

½ (2-oz size) package onion soup mix (1 envelope)
½ cup water
1 (10½-oz) can condensed golden mushroom soup

Spray 4- to 5-quart slow cooker with cooking spray and place pork chops in slow cooker. Layer with onions and mushrooms. Combine soup mix, water, and soup and pour over mushrooms. Cover and cook on low heat for 6 to 8 hours or until pork is tender. Makes 4 servings.

He that is of a merry heart hath a continual feast.
PROVERBS 15:15 KJV

Give us merry hearts, Lord.

STEW PROVENÇAL

2 cans (about 14 oz each) beef broth, divided
$\frac{1}{3}$ cup all-purpose flour
$1\frac{1}{2}$ lbs pork tenderloin, trimmed and diced
4 red potatoes, unpeeled, cut into cubes

2 cups frozen cut green beans
1 onion, chopped
2 cloves garlic, minced
1 tsp salt
1 tsp dried thyme leaves
$\frac{1}{2}$ tsp black pepper

Mix $\frac{1}{2}$ cup beef broth and flour in a small bowl; set aside. Add remaining broth and rest of ingredients to slow cooker and stir. Cover and cook on low 8 to 10 hours or on high 4 to 5 hours. Stir in flour mixture and cook an additional 30 minutes to thicken. Serves 8.

Physical and biological food. . .
is only a small portion of the food Jesus has to offer to those that come to Him.
The kind of food that Jesus is offering is the food of His everlasting life.

ROBERT FABING

May each physical meal I make,
God, remind me of the eternal meal You serve through Jesus Christ.

Love Offerings

Our world rates the value of our work according to our success or failure. Surrounded constantly by this mindset, we can't help but absorb this way of thinking. We feel good about ourselves when we accomplish a lot, when we're well organized and efficient, when others are impressed with our efforts. But when we fall behind, when we can't seem to work very fast, when our efforts don't seem to measure up to that of those around us, we may lose confidence in ourselves; we may even feel we're less valuable to God.

But God doesn't see with the world's eyes. When we cook supper for our families, He doesn't care if the potatoes are hard or the rice burned—and He doesn't mind if the kitchen floor needs mopping and the stove is greasy. All He wants is for us to offer everything up to Him—potatoes, kitchen floors, greasy stoves, the whole kit and caboodle. He treasures even the most insignificant love offerings.

On the days when our kitchen routines tick smoothly along, our Lord is delighted by the shining countertops and the fragrant aromas of home-cooked meals. But He delights in us every bit as much on those days when our lives—and our kitchens—have fallen into shambles.

Each meal we serve our families can truly be an offering of love—not only to our families but to Jesus. Lovers express themselves in tangible ways. If we say we love Jesus, then we need to show Him that we do. Obviously, we can't cook Him a meal.

But we can cook one for our children.

101 Easy Supper Ideas

I was hungry, and you fed me.
MATTHEW 25:35 NLT

Feed my sheep.
JOHN 21:16

Dearest Lord, may I see You, today and every day, in the person of [my family], and whilst [cooking for] them, minister unto You. . . . May I recognize You, and say, "Jesus. . .how sweet it is to serve You."

    Lord, give me this seeing faith, then my work will never be monotonous. . . . Sweetest Lord, make me appreciative of the dignity of my high vocation and its many responsibilities. Never permit me to disgrace it by giving way to coldness, unkindness, or impatience.

    . . .Lord, increase my faith, bless my efforts and work, now and for evermore.

adapted from the workers' prayer at
MOTHER TERESA'S orphanage in Calcutta

3-CHEESE CHICKEN & NOODLES

3 cups chopped cooked chicken
1½ cups cottage cheese
1 (10½-oz) can condensed cream of
   chicken soup, undiluted
1 (8-oz) package wide egg noodles,
   cooked and drained
1 cup grated Monterey Jack cheese
½ cup chicken broth
½ tsp dried thyme leaves

½ cup diced celery
½ cup diced onion
½ cup diced green bell pepper
½ cup diced red bell pepper
½ cup grated Parmesan cheese
1 (4-oz) can sliced mushrooms,
   drained
2 tbsp butter, melted

Mix all ingredients together in slow cooker, stirring to coat evenly. Cover and cook on low 6 to 10 hours. Serves 6.

A feast is made for laughter.
ECCLESIASTES 10:19 KJV

Fill our meals with laughter, Lord.

FIESTA RICE AND SAUSAGE

1 tsp vegetable oil
2 lbs spicy Italian sausage,
  casing removed
2 cloves garlic, minced
2 tsp ground cumin
4 onions, chopped

4 green bell peppers, chopped
3 jalapeño peppers, seeded
  and minced
4 cups beef broth
2 (6½-oz) packages long-grain
  and wild rice mix

Heat oil in large skillet. Cook sausage for about 5 minutes or until browned, breaking apart with back of spoon. Add garlic and cumin; cook 30 seconds. Add onions, bell peppers, and jalapeño peppers and sauté about 10 minutes or until onions are tender. Spoon mixture into slow cooker. Add beef broth and rice; cover and cook on low 4 to 6 hours. Makes 10 to 12 servings.

*God loves us—loves us so much that the divine presence
is revealed even in the meaningless workings of daily life. . . .
Seen in this light, what strikes many modern readers as the ludicrous attention to detail
in the book of Leviticus, involving God in the minutiae of daily life—
all the cooking and cleaning of a people's domestic life—
might be revisioned as the very love of God.*

KATHLEEN NORRIS

**Thank You, God,
for paying attention to even the smallest details of my day.**

Tuna Casserole

2 (12-oz) cans tuna, drained
   and flaked
3 cups diced celery
3 cups crushed potato chips, divided
6 hard-cooked eggs, chopped
1 (10½-oz) can condensed cream
   of mushroom soup, undiluted

1 (10½-oz) can condensed cream
   of celery soup, undiluted
1 cup mayonnaise
1 tsp dried tarragon leaves
1 tsp black pepper

Stir together all ingredients except ½ cup potato chips in slow cooker; mix well. Sprinkle remaining ½ cup potato chips on top. Cover and cook on low 5 to 8 hours. Makes 8 servings.

And I will fetch a morsel of bread, and comfort ye your hearts.
GENESIS 18:5 KJV

Today, Lord, and every day, I need Your comfort.

Be ye kind one to another. . .forgiving one another,
even as God for Christ's sake hath forgiven you.
EPHESIANS 4:32 KJV

A Feast of Forgiveness

When I think of cooking as one more chore in my already full day, then I miss an opportunity for joy. Meals give us a chance to relax and enjoy each other. They allow us time to laugh and exchange ideas. And maybe most of all they are opportunities for reconciliation.

Look not every man on his own things,

but every man also on the things of others.

Let this mind be in you,

which was also in Christ Jesus.

PHILIPPIANS 2:4–5 KJV

CHEESY PORK AND POTATOES

½ lb ground pork, cooked and crumbled
½ cup finely crushed saltine crackers
⅓ cup barbecue sauce
1 egg
3 tbsp margarine
1 tbsp vegetable oil
4 potatoes, peeled and thinly sliced

1 onion, thinly sliced
1 cup grated mozzarella cheese
⅔ cup evaporated milk
1 tsp salt
½ tsp paprika
⅛ tsp black pepper
chopped parsley

In a large bowl, combine pork, crackers, barbecue sauce, and egg; shape mixture into 6 patties. In medium skillet, heat margarine and oil; sauté potatoes and onion until lightly browned. Drain and place in slow cooker. Mix together cheese, milk, salt, paprika, and pepper in small bowl. Pour into slow cooker over potatoes. Layer pork patties on top. Cover and cook on low for 3 to 5 hours. Garnish with parsley. Makes 6 servings.

"I am the food," is what Jesus is saying. . . .
Jesus is crying out that what human beings hunger for is Him, His love, His person. . . .
This is food that will last.
"Why spend your wages on what fails to satisfy?" (Isaiah 55)
ROBERT FABING

**Help me not to forget, dear Lord,
that You alone can truly satisfy the hunger of my heart.**

ITALIAN MEAT LOAF

1 (8-oz) can tomato sauce, divided
1 egg, lightly beaten
½ cup chopped onion
½ cup chopped green bell pepper
⅓ cup dry seasoned bread crumbs
2 tbsp grated Parmesan cheese

½ tsp garlic powder
½ tsp black pepper
1 lb ground beef
½ lb ground pork or veal
1 cup shredded Asiago cheese

Set aside ⅓ cup tomato sauce in refrigerator. Mix remaining tomato sauce and egg in large bowl. Stir in onion, bell pepper, bread crumbs, Parmesan cheese, garlic powder, and black pepper. Mix in ground beef and pork; shape into a loaf. Place meat loaf on foil handles (see below) and lower into slow cooker. Cover and cook on low 8 to 10 hours; remove when internal temperature reads 170°F. Spread reserved tomato sauce over meat loaf and sprinkle with Asiago cheese. Cover and cook another 15 minutes, or until cheese is melted. Remove meat loaf from slow cooker using foil handles.

To make foil handles: Tear off three 18x2-inch strips of heavy foil or use regular foil folded to double thickness. Crisscross foil strips in spoke design and place in slow cooker to make lifting meat loaf easier.

Behold, I will rain bread from heaven for you.
EXODUS 16:4 KJV

Why do I worry so much about the everyday details of my life, Lord, when You have promised to give me food from heaven?

94

TURKEY MUSHROOM STEW

1 lb turkey cutlets, cut into 4x1-inch
   strips
1 small yellow onion, thinly sliced
2 tbsp minced green onions with tops
$\frac{1}{2}$ lb mushrooms, sliced
2 to 3 tbsp flour
1 cup half-and-half or milk

1 tsp dried tarragon leaves
1 tsp salt
black pepper to taste
$\frac{1}{2}$ cup frozen peas
$\frac{1}{2}$ cup sour cream (optional)
puff pastry shells

Place onions, mushrooms, and turkey in slow cooker. Cover and cook on low 4 hours. Pour turkey and vegetables into serving bowl and turn slow cooker up to high setting. Stir flour into half-and-half until smooth; pour into slow cooker. Add tarragon, salt, and pepper. Return cooked vegetables and turkey to slow cooker and stir in peas. Cover and cook 1 hour or until sauce has thickened and peas are heated through. Just before serving stir in sour cream, if desired. Serve in puff pastry shells. Makes 4 servings.

Look at all that happened at the meal Jesus had with Zacchaeus.
Look at all the real food, all of the intimacy,
all of the satisfaction, and all of the fulfillment.
This is the real food of Jesus.

ROBERT FABING

**Please, Jesus, come and eat supper with us tonight,
just like You did with Zacchaeus.**

Be kindly affectioned one to another with brotherly love;
in honour preferring one another.
ROMANS 12:10 KJV

Plenty for Everyone

When my brother and I were young, we fought constantly over food. We were each always sure that the other was going to get more—and as a result, if we had to share a candy bar, we practically used a protractor to divide it into equal halves. In the same way, we carefully counted out the cherries or berries, to make sure we each had the same amount in our individual bowls. I'm ashamed to admit that sometimes, after the fruit had already been counted and agreed upon, I would smuggle a bite from my brother's bowl. I felt no shame at the time, however, merely a smug triumph that I had beat him for once.

Store-bought treats, strangely enough, were highly valued by my brother and me, since my mother did most of her own baking herself. Once in a while, we would be given a single package of Hostess Ho-Hos, and we treated these sugary delights as though they were treasure. Since the package held only two cupcakes, they were easy enough for us to divide fairly. On one occasion, though, my brother had an upset stomach when I ate my share, so his cupcake was left for a later meal.

The next day I came home from school and found the house empty. I went to the cupboard to get myself a snack—and there was that single cupcake, waiting for my brother. I tried to ignore it. But the moist chocolate frosting and creamy filling called to me. Before I could think, I had stuffed it into my mouth.

101 Easy Supper Ideas

My brother was loudly indignant when he discovered his cupcake was gone. I denied that I had touched it. He insisted I must have. My mother wondered if someone had wandered into the house and eaten the cupcake. My brother rolled his eyes at this hypothesis, still certain that I was the guilty party. I protested my innocence so firmly, however, that my mother was convinced. Much to my brother's disgust and frustration, the "mystery" of the missing cupcake was never solved.

Several years later when we were both teenagers, my brother died in a plane crash. By then we had resolved some of our intense sibling rivalry—but I had never told him the truth about that cupcake.

Several months ago, though, I dreamed that my brother and I were sharing a meal. In the meal, I knew he was dead, but somehow we were being allowed a "visit." We talked about my children throughout the meal, and then as we finished the food, my brother asked me what was for dessert. I reached into my purse and pulled out a Hostess Ho-Ho. "Here," I said. "I owe you this."

"There's plenty for us both," he answered. "Let's share."

The dream lingered in my mind for days, giving me a sense of joy. I carried it with me to the supper table every night, as I listened to my children squabble over their food, just as my brother and I had once done. "It's not fair," I heard them say over and over. "She has more than me. It's not fair."

I'm not sure how I can convince them that when we stop worrying so much about "fair," we'll find there really is enough for us all. The only thing I know to do is to try to demonstrate with my own life a willingness to share, a readiness to forgive.

Each meal we share as a family is precious; each is a practical, tangible opportunity to put another's desires before our own, a chance to be reconciled in love with one another.

i have noticed
that when
chickens quit
quarreling over their
food they often
find that there is
enough for all of them
i wonder if
it might not
be the same way
with the
human race

HARRY EMERSON FOSDICK

BBQ Pork Sandwiches

4 lbs boneless pork loin roast
1 can (14½ oz) beef broth
⅓ cup Worcestershire sauce
⅓ cup hot sauce (less if your family doesn't like "hot")

SAUCE
½ cup ketchup   ½ cup yellow mustard
½ cup molasses   ½ cup Worcestershire sauce

Combine sauce ingredients in a large bowl and set aside. Place roast on bottom of slow cooker. Mix together broth, Worcestershire sauce, and hot sauce; pour over roast. Cover and cook on low for 10 hours or until roast is tender. Place roast on large cutting board; dispose of liquid. Chop roast and stir into reserved sauce. Spoon pork mixture on large rolls and serve with potato salad. Makes 8 to 10 servings.

Repetition is the daily bread which satisfies with benediction.
SOREN KIERKEGAARD

**Remind me, Christ Jesus, that in the routine repetition of my life
You give me Your blessings.**

SLOPPY JOES

3 lbs lean ground beef
1 cup chopped onion
3 cloves garlic, minced
1½ cups ketchup
1 cup chopped red bell pepper
5 tbsp Worcestershire sauce

4 tbsp brown sugar
3 tbsp vinegar
3 tbsp mustard
2 tsp chili powder
hamburger buns

Brown onion, garlic, and beef in large skillet; drain excess fat. Mix together ketchup, bell pepper, Worcestershire sauce, brown sugar, vinegar, mustard, and chili powder in slow cooker; stir in beef mixture. Cover and cook on low 6 to 8 hours. Spoon onto hamburger buns. Makes 8 to 10 servings.

I had never thought about the. . .
obvious fact that preparing a meal can be a sign of
caring and loving communication.
RUTH HUBBARD

**Each night when I serve the meal, Lord,
help me to think about what I am communicating to my family.**

CLASSIC BEEF & NOODLES

2 lbs beef stew meat, trimmed and cut
   into cubes
½ lb mushrooms, sliced into halves
2 tbsp chopped onion
2 cloves garlic, minced
1 tsp salt
1 tsp dried oregano leaves
½ tsp black pepper

½ tsp dried marjoram leaves
1 bay leaf
1½ cups beef broth
1 (8-oz) container sour cream
½ cup all-purpose flour
½ cup water
4 cups hot cooked noodles

Place beef, mushrooms, onion, garlic, salt, oregano, pepper, marjoram, and bay leaf in slow cooker. Add beef broth; cover and cook on low 8 to 10 hours. Remove and discard bay leaf. Turn slow cooker to high. Mix sour cream, flour, and water together in small bowl. Add about 1 cup liquid from slow cooker to sour cream mixture. Blend and pour back into slow cooker. Cover and cook on high about 30 minutes or until thickened and bubbly. Serve over noodles. Makes 8 servings.

And ye shall serve the LORD your God, and he shall bless thy bread.
EXODUS 23:25 KJV

**Thank You for all Your blessings,
God. Help us each to serve You with our whole hearts.**

CHICKEN Á LA KING

1 (10½-oz) can condensed cream of
   chicken soup, undiluted
3 tbsp all-purpose flour
½ tsp pepper
dash cayenne pepper
1 lb boneless, skinless chicken breasts,
   cut into cubes

1 celery rib, chopped
½ cup chopped green pepper
½ cup chopped onion
1 (10-oz) package frozen peas,
   thawed
2 tbsp diced pimientos, drained
hot cooked rice

In a slow cooker, combine soup, flour, pepper, and cayenne until smooth. Stir in chicken, celery, green pepper, and onion. Cover and cook on low for 7–8 hours or until meat juices run clear. Stir in peas and pimientos. Cook 30 minutes longer or until heated through. Serve over rice. Makes 6 servings.

True service will not seek recognition from those at the table,
only from the one who's preparing an eternal banquet for us.
And as we live simply as Christ-bearers,
our faith in action, our creative "kitchen work,"
will naturally reflect the ultimate Servant. . . .

JO KADLECEK

**As I serve my family, dear Jesus,
remind me that I'm following in Your footsteps.**

Last-Minute Inspiration:

One-Pan Dishes and Stir-Fry Meals

When I was studying Greek in college,
our professor pointed out to us an interesting thought
in the story of Jesus, Mary, and Martha.
Where Jesus said, "But one thing is needful,"
our professor suggested that might just as well be translated,
"But one dish is needful."
Obviously Martha was laying it on, and Jesus was suggesting she keep it simple.
Some of the sweetest fellowship can be had around the simplest of meals.

RUTH GRAHAM BELL

Simple Pleasures

"More is better." Those words might as well be our national motto. (Hopefully, we'll never inscribe it on our coins in place of "In God we trust.") We all buy into this philosophy at many levels. One way to simplify our lives is to refuse to accept this as our motto any longer.

When it comes to cooking supper, a quick, one-pan meal can be just as nutritious as an elaborate four-course dinner—and it can leave our families more time for shared moments of serenity and joy. Simple ways are often best.

Sometimes I take on more than I really need to do. I get so busy, so focused on all that I *have* to do, that my sense of perspective disappears. Times like that I need to make time to simply breathe, to step back and evaluate my life. When I do, I often find that some of my routines can be pared down; that someone else might be able to do part of the work I've been doing all by myself; that the world will not end if I don't do everything.

Making sure that the whole family participates in kitchen chores is one way to simplify your life as a mother. Another is to use the recipes that follow for quick, one-pan or stir-fry meals. These recipes are particularly good for those evenings when you *haven't* thought ahead, when you need a little last-minute inspiration.

JUGGLING TIP:
Divvy up the kitchen chores.
No rule says that the mother has to do them all—
and even the youngest child is capable of helping.
From making the grocery list to
setting the table to cleaning up after the meal,
if you all share in the work,
you'll all be done that much sooner—
leaving your family more time for other things.

RANCH CLAM CHOWDER

½ cup chopped onion
3 tbsp butter or margarine
½ lb fresh mushrooms, sliced
2 tbsp Worcestershire sauce
1½ cups half-and-half
1 (10½-oz) can cream of
   potato soup

1 (1-oz) package ranch salad
   dressing mix
1 (10-oz) can whole baby clams,
   undrained
chopped parsley

Sauté onion in butter in a 3-quart saucepan until soft, but not browned. Add mushrooms and Worcestershire sauce; cook until mushrooms are soft and pan juices have almost evaporated. In medium bowl, whisk together potato soup, salad dressing mix, and half-and-half until smooth. Drain clam liquid into dressing mixture and stir into mushrooms in pan. Cook uncovered until soup is heated through but not boiling. Add clams to soup; heat through again. Garnish with parsley before serving.

Food is to kids what music is to singers.
It is. . .a communication form, it is an event and an experience.
It is a security blanket, it is learning, it is thought, it is habit. . . .
Food is life and love and sustenance.
It represents a large part of all the child knows about love and care.
ANITA BRYANT

Lord, may my children always know how much they are loved.

CHICKEN NOODLE SOUP EXPRESS

2 (14$\frac{1}{2}$-oz) cans chicken broth
generous dash pepper
1 medium carrot, sliced (about $\frac{1}{2}$ cup)
1 stalk celery, sliced (about $\frac{1}{2}$ cup)
$\frac{1}{2}$ cup uncooked medium egg noodles
1 (5-oz) can chunk chicken, drained,
    or $\frac{1}{2}$ cup chopped leftover chicken from
    an earlier meal

Mix broth, pepper, carrot, and celery in medium saucepan over medium-high heat and bring to a boil. Stir in noodles and reduce heat to medium. Cook about 10 minutes, stirring frequently. Add chicken and heat through. Makes 4 servings.

The truth is that at the end of a well-savored meal
both soul and body enjoy a special well-being. . . .
JEAN ANTHELME BRILLAT-SAVARIN

Dear Lord, You bless me in so many ways.
My soul and body are healthy because of You.

Meaty Chili

1 lb coarsely ground beef	1 (12-oz) can tomato juice
½ lb ground Italian sausage	1 cup water
1 large onion, chopped	½ cup ketchup
2 medium ribs celery, diced	1 tsp sugar
2 fresh jalapeño peppers, chopped	1 tsp chili powder
2 cloves garlic, minced	½ tsp salt
1 (28-oz) can whole peeled tomatoes, undrained, cut up	½ tsp ground cumin
	½ tsp dried thyme leaves
1 (15-oz) can pinto beans, drained	⅛ tsp black pepper

Place beef, sausage, onion, celery, jalapeños, and garlic in a 5-quart Dutch oven and cook over medium-high heat until meat is browned and onion is tender, stirring frequently. Stir in remaining ingredients and bring to a boil over high heat. Reduce heat to medium-low and simmer uncovered for 30 minutes, stirring occasionally. Serves 6.

Until I was twelve, I thought spaghetti came from a can,
and that vegetables grew in the freezer.
When I discovered that green beans grew in the ground, I thought it was a miracle.

Mollie Katzen

Help us, Lord,
to see the miracle of Your grace even in ordinary things—
like green beans fresh from the garden.

THAI GINGER CHICKEN & VEGETABLES

1 (8-oz) package Thai rice noodles (or dried linguini)
1 lb boneless, skinless chicken breast halves, cut into pieces
1 cup Thai ginger marinade
3 tbsp butter
2 cups bite-sized broccoli florets
2 cups bite-sized cauliflower florets
½ medium (1 cup) red pepper, cut into strips
1 cup chicken broth
2 tbsp water
1 tbsp cornstarch

Cook noodles according to package directions. Drain; keep warm. In large resealable plastic food bag, combine chicken pieces and ½ cup marinade. Seal tightly. Turn several times to coat well. Place in 13x9-inch pan and refrigerate at least 30 minutes. In a 12-inch skillet melt 2 tablespoons butter until sizzling. Cook broccoli, cauliflower, and red pepper over medium-high heat for 5 to 7 minutes, or until vegetables are crisp but tender, stirring occasionally. Remove from skillet. Melt remaining butter in skillet and add chicken mixture. Cook 4 to 6 minutes until chicken is no longer pink, stirring occasionally. Cook another 3 to 5 minutes to bring mixture to a boil. In a small bowl, stir together water and cornstarch; stir into chicken mixture to thicken. Add remaining ½ cup marinade and continue cooking 3 to 5 minutes until mixture comes to a boil. Add cooked noodles and vegetables to chicken mixture; toss to coat lightly. Makes 6 servings.

The bread which we break, is it not the communion of the body of Christ?
For we being many are one bread, and one body:
for we are all partakers of that one bread.
1 CORINTHIANS 10:16–17 KJV

———————

Jesus, remind us as we eat our earthly bread,
that You are the spiritual bread for the entire world.

Strange to see how a good dinner and feasting reconciles everybody.
SAMUEL PEPYS, 1633–1703

An Open Heart

I walked fast along the beach, tears in my eyes. My husband and I had just had another fight, and I wanted to get as far as possible away from him. Life was much easier when I was alone, I told myself, my blood beating hard with anger.

Gradually, though, the ocean's roar and sigh quieted me. In front of me, the foam glowed white against the blue night that had fallen across the water. I sat on the sand and watched the moon rise out of the ocean, an orange wafer that cast a million dancing streaks. I sighed, feeling a quiet Presence creep into my heart.

The Presence seemed to be nudging me to get up and leave this peaceful spot. "I don't want to go back," I whispered. "I want to be alone with You." But the gentle Presence persisted, and I got to my feet.

As I drew closer to our house, though, I walked slower. I didn't want to go inside. I had too long a list of grievances. I knew it was suppertime, and the children would be hungry, but that fact was at the top of my list: Why couldn't my husband make supper for a change? Why was everything always my job?

When did we get to this cold, angry place? I wondered. When did my lover and my best friend turn into my enemy? My heart felt as tight as a fist, but I drew in a deep breath and opened the door.

A burst of warmth and light and good smells made me blink. The table was spread with food, and the kids were already sitting down. My husband was at the stove, dishing up the last plate. "You're just in time," he said. His voice was full of apology and welcome.

I couldn't meet his eyes as I sat down; I was still too angry to throw away my grievance list. But as I sat across from him, eating the good food he'd made, listening to our children's voices, I couldn't help but remember another meal we'd shared.

That day, all our friends and family had shared the food with us. Bright balloons danced in the air behind our chairs, flowers decorated the tables, and I wore a long lace gown. When my eyes had met my husband's, our gaze was full of promises.

What had changed since then? I glanced around the table at our three kids, and my mouth twitched; for one thing, our "guests" were different today. As I looked at the children's worried faces, though, I realized that in a sense they *were* our guests—and what a rude, self-centered hostess I had been lately.

Something was knocking at my heart's closed door, asking patiently to come in. I thought of the quiet Presence I had sought beside the ocean; He couldn't live within me, I realized, if I was too proud to open my heart again to my husband. I smiled at my children, and my heart began to unfurl. At last, I looked across the table and into my husband's eyes.

His gaze held the same promise it had on our wedding day. And my heart opened wide in welcome.

Here I am! I stand at the door and knock.
If anyone hears my voice and opens the door,
I will come in and eat with him, and he with me.

REVELATION 3:20

Blessed are those who
are invited to the wedding supper
of the Lamb!

REVELATION 19:9

LEMON-DILL SALMON WITH RED POTATOES

½ cup water
1 lb (4 cups) new red potatoes, cut into
    1-inch pieces
1 lb salmon fillet
1 tbsp chopped fresh dill (or 1 tsp dried
    dill weed)

1½ cups fresh pea pods
2 tbsp fresh lemon juice
1 tsp cornstarch
½ tsp salt
½ cup apple juice

Cook water and potatoes over high heat in a 12-inch skillet for 2 to 3 minutes, or until mixture comes to a boil. Reduce heat to low; cover and cook 10 minutes. Layer salmon fillet over potatoes; add apple juice and dill. Cover and continue cooking about 10 to 12 minutes, until fish flakes with fork. Add pea pods; cover and continue cooking 2 to 4 minutes, or until peas are tender. Remove skin from salmon; break into chunks. In a small bowl, blend lemon juice and cornstarch. Stir into salmon and potato mixture. Cook 3 to 5 minutes over medium-high heat until mixture comes to a boil, stirring occasionally. Season with salt. Makes 4 servings.

Bring mindfulness to whatever it is that you're doing each moment.
If you're doing physical work, stop and consider the food.
Think about it. Look at the food. Where did it come from?

ROBERT BRYANT

Remind me, God, not to take any of Your blessings for granted.
Help me to really see the wonder of Your love whenever I
prepare food, eat a meal. . .or even clean the kitchen.

CHICKEN WITH CASHEWS

2 tbsp butter
1 tsp chili puree with garlic
½ lb precut chicken stir-fry meat
½ cup teriyaki sauce

1 (16-oz) package fresh
   stir-fry vegetables
½ cup salted cashews
2 cups hot cooked couscous

In a 10-inch skillet or wok, melt butter until sizzling; stir in chili puree. Add chicken and cook over medium-high heat 5 to 7 minutes until chicken is no longer pink, stirring occasionally. Add teriyaki sauce and vegetables. Continue to cook 5 to 6 minutes until vegetables are tender but still crisp, stirring constantly. Stir in cashews. Serve over couscous. Makes 4 servings.

The act of [Communion] begins with breaking open our lives.
To take time to care and prepare a nurtured and beautiful meal—
this is also a breaking open of my being, my wisdom, my understanding. . .
to provide for my family.
Even the aroma of different foods is welcome and satisfying.
JEAN MOLESKY-POZ

Break open my life, Lord Jesus.
Use my hands as I provide food for my family.
May I never be so busy I miss the welcome,
satisfying aroma of Your presence.

ITALIAN MINESTRONE BOWLS

10 oz uncooked, dried spaghetti, broken in half
1 tbsp butter
½ lb boneless, skinless chicken breast halves, cut into 1-inch pieces
1 tbsp dried Italian seasoning (or ½ tsp *each* dried oregano leaves, dried marjoram leaves, dried basil leaves, and rubbed sage)
1 tsp finely chopped fresh garlic
2 (14½-oz) cans low-sodium chicken broth
1 (16-oz) package frozen vegetable combination
1 (15-oz) can cannellini beans, drained

Cook spaghetti according to package directions. Drain; keep warm. Melt butter in 4-quart saucepan until sizzling. Cook chicken, seasoning, and garlic over medium-high heat for 5 to 6 minutes, or until chicken is no longer pink, stirring occasionally. Add broth, vegetables, and beans; continue cooking 8 to 10 minutes until heated through, stirring occasionally. Divide spaghetti among serving bowls and pour chicken mixture over top. Makes 6 servings.

Everything that is good in life is a gift from God, including the food we eat.
We may have gone out and worked all week so that we could buy it,
but God is the one who gave us the job, the strength or ability to work.
CLAYTON HARROP

Thank You, God, for all Your wonderful gifts.

GERMAN GOULASH

1 lb beef stew meat, cut into bite-sized pieces
2 tbsp all-purpose flour
2 tbsp butter
1 medium onion, quartered, sliced
1½ cups water
⅓ cup tomato puree
1 medium green pepper, quartered, sliced

2 tsp instant beef bouillon
1 tsp paprika
1 (12-oz) package (4 cups) frozen cooked spaetzle (or uncooked dried dumpling noodles)
sour cream, if desired
chopped fresh parsley, if desired

Melt butter in Dutch oven until sizzling; add flour-coated beef pieces, and cook over medium-high heat until browned (5 to 6 minutes). Add remaining flour and onion; continue to cook until lightly browned (2 to 3 minutes). Stir in water, tomato puree, green pepper, bouillon, and paprika; cover and cook, bringing to a boil (2 to 3 minutes). Reduce to low heat. Cook 1 to 1½ hours, until meat is tender, stirring once or twice. Cover and allow to stand 5 minutes. Heat spaetzle (or cook noodles) according to package directions; divide among serving bowls. Cover with meat mixture and top with sour cream and parsley if desired. Makes 4 servings.

Let us eat, and be merry.
LUKE 15:23 KJV

Jesus, make our meals happy times, filled with conversation and laughter and love.

Pass It On

When I'm rushed and busy, little things seem so important—a forgotten chore, a spilled water glass, a misunderstood word. If I want my children to learn that each meal can be an opportunity for forgiveness, however, then they must see that same open attitude in my own life. I must be quick to say I'm sorry when I'm wrong—and just as quick to forgive when another is in the wrong. When we say grace before the meal, not only do we need to thank God for our food, but we also need to thank Him for His forgiveness, reminding each other to pass along the same forgiveness Jesus offers us.

Even as Christ forgave you,

so also do ye.

COLOSSIANS 3:13 KJV

SOUTHEAST ASIAN LO MEIN

3 cups cubed cooked pork (or chicken)
2 cups julienne-cut carrots
1 cup water
2 (14½-oz) cans chicken broth
½ (10-oz) package frozen chopped spinach, thawed
6 green onions, sliced
2 tbsp soy sauce
1 tsp Chinese five-spice powder
1 (8-oz) package lo mein noodles (or 8 oz uncooked dried spaghetti)

Place all ingredients except lo mein noodles in 3-quart saucepan. Cover and cook over medium-high heat until mixture comes to a boil (6 to 7 minutes). Reduce heat to low; cook until carrots are tender (8 to 10 minutes). Cook noodles according to package directions; drain well. Divide noodles among bowls and pour vegetable-meat broth over noodles. Makes 6 servings.

[Jesus] said to them: Have you any food here?
So they gave him a piece of a broiled fish and some honeycomb,
and he took it and ate it.
LUKE 24:41–43 NKJV

Thank You, Jesus, that You lived on earth in a human body.
You felt hunger; You enjoyed good food. You understand us.

ITALIAN CHICKEN CACCIATORE

2 tbsp butter
1 (3- to 4-lb) frying chicken, cut into 8 pieces, skinned
2 (14½-oz) cans Italian-style diced tomatoes
1 (4-oz) can sliced mushrooms, drained
1 medium onion, cut into eighths
1 medium green pepper, cut into ½-inch pieces
½ tsp salt
½ tsp pepper
1 (9-oz) package refrigerated fresh fettuccini, cut in half

In 12-inch skillet melt butter until sizzling; cook chicken pieces over medium-high heat until browned (10 to 12 minutes), turning once. Add remaining ingredients except fettuccini. Cover and cook 30 to 40 minutes until chicken is no longer pink. Stir in fettuccini just before serving; cover and cook 6 to 9 minutes until fettuccini is tender. Makes 8 servings.

And God said, Behold, I have given you every herb bearing seed,
which is upon the face of all the earth, and every tree,
in the which is the fruit of a tree yielding seed; to you it shall be for meat.
GENESIS 1:29 KJV

God, I am grateful for all the ways You feed me.

BURGERS ITALIANO

2 lbs lean ground beef
1 (10-oz) package frozen chopped
   spinach, thawed and well-drained
2 cloves garlic, finely chopped

½ cup grated Parmesan cheese
1 cup prepared spaghetti sauce
½ cup packaged Italian-seasoned
   bread crumbs

Heat broiler or outdoor gas grill to hot. Mix all ingredients well in a large bowl. Divide into 8 equal portions and shape into patties. Broil or grill 6 minutes on each side until cooked through, keeping 4 inches from heat. Serve with antipasto salad. Makes 8 burgers.

*Cooking that comes from the soul. . .
comes from what you know,
what your grandmother taught you.
It's good because it's cooked with love.*

CLARA OLIVER

Lord, may all my food be cooked with love.

Finding Our Spiritual Sustenance So We Can Feed Others

*It is a balanced meal that Jesus serves us,
a feast that, in turn, gives us balance to serve others.*
Jo Kadlecek

**In God's name I beseech you let prayer nourish your soul
as your meals nourish your body.**
E. M. Bounds

If you have come up with a plan for mealtimes, one that involves the whole family's help, if you have helped yourself to the recipes like those offered in this book as a way to make your cooking quicker and more efficient, and yet you still find that meal preparation is one of the heaviest balls you juggle, then maybe you need to set aside some time to see just why this particular ball seems so heavy.

- Has your life become unbalanced in some other area?
- Does making time for meal preparation seem impossible because you're

actually impossibly overcommitted somewhere else?
- Are you in fact trying to keep too many balls up in the air at once?
- Do you take time for yourself?
- Is there some small space in each day when you spend time with God alone?

> LET US PUT OURSELVES COMPLETELY UNDER THE POWER AND INFLUENCE OF JESUS, SO THAT HE MAY THINK WITH OUR MINDS, WORK WITH OUR HANDS, FOR WE CAN DO ALL THINGS IF HIS STRENGTH IS WITH US.
> MOTHER TERESA

I find that my juggling routine is not something I can ever hope to get perfect; it may go along smoothly for days, even weeks or months at a time —and then, almost imperceptibly, I find myself juggling more frantically, making more mistakes, dropping more balls. The routine just isn't working anymore. That's when I need to stop everything and create an opportunity to be alone, time to pray and ask God for His help as I reevaluate my life. I need to take time to nourish my own soul.

If we are to offer the members of our families balanced meals day after day, then we need to help ourselves to the balanced spiritual nutrition Jesus longs to serve us.

CHEESE CAULIFLOWER SOUP

9 scallions, chopped
1 tbsp olive oil
4 cups chicken broth
2 (8-oz) packages fresh
    cauliflower flowerets

$\frac{1}{2}$ cup all-purpose flour
$1\frac{1}{2}$ cups shredded pepper-Jack cheese
$\frac{1}{2}$ cup bottled roasted red peppers
$\frac{1}{2}$ tsp salt (optional)
$\frac{1}{2}$ tsp hot-pepper sauce

Place scallions in oil in medium saucepan and sauté 3 minutes. Add 3 cups broth and bring to boiling; add cauliflower and return to boiling. Reduce heat to medium and cook 6 more minutes, or until almost tender. In a small bowl, whisk together flour and remaining 1 cup chicken broth. Pour into saucepan and bring to a boil, stirring occasionally until thickened (about 2 to 3 minutes). Remove soup from heat and stir in cheese, roasted red peppers, salt, and hot-pepper sauce, breaking up red peppers with a wooden spoon. Makes 4 servings.

Good cooks worked with their whole heart,
doing the best they could with what they had on hand
to make sure that their dishes would be enjoyed
by all who sat down to eat.

EVAN JONES

**No matter how simple a meal I make, dear Lord,
may I cook with my whole heart.**

SKILLET CHICKEN AND RICE

1 tbsp olive oil
1 sweet green pepper, cored, seeded, and diced
1 cup frozen chopped onion
1 (5-oz) package yellow rice mix
1 (14.5-oz) can Mexican-style stewed tomatoes, diced
1½ cups water

1 lb chicken tenders or boneless, skinless chicken breast halves
½ tsp salt
½ cup drained canned pinto beans, rinsed
½ cup sliced pitted green olives
½ tsp liquid hot-pepper sauce
½ to ⅔ cup chopped fresh cilantro

In a large, nonstick skillet cook pepper and onion in oil over medium heat, stirring for 4 minutes. Stir in rice mix, tomatoes, and water; simmer, covered, for 10 minutes. Salt chicken and add to rice along with beans, olives, and hot-pepper sauce. Cook covered for 8 to 10 minutes, or until rice is tender. Sprinkle with cilantro. Makes 4 servings.

Including a pinch of love is the secret to "doin' it right."
DEBORAH KESTEN

No matter how hectic my day, God, remind me not to leave out the "pinch of love."

New York Reuben

4 slices deli-style seeded rye bread
1 (1-lb) refrigerated bag sauerkraut, drained
4 tbsp Thousand Island dressing, plus extra for serving
½ lb thinly sliced corned beef (about 12 slices)
½ lb thinly sliced Swiss cheese (about 8 slices)

Heat broiler and coat broiler-pan rack with nonstick cooking spray. Toast bread in broiler. In a small saucepan, gently heat sauerkraut. Spread 1 tablespoon dressing over each slice of bread and top with corned beef, sauerkraut, and Swiss cheese. Broil for 3 minutes 4 to 6 inches from heat until tops are lightly browned and cheese is melted. Serve immediately with extra Thousand Island dressing on the side. Makes 4 sandwiches.

Sharing food and fellowship ultimately also has a lot to do with your relationship to God.
CLAYTON HARROP

May our food and fellowship always draw us closer to You, dear Lord.

HONEY-MUSTARD CHICKEN

3 tbsp packaged unflavored bread
   crumbs
1 tsp chili powder
1 lb boneless, skinless chicken thighs
1 tbsp olive oil
$\frac{1}{2}$ cup honey mustard

1 cup milk
1 tbsp all-purpose flour
$\frac{1}{2}$ tsp salt
2 cups shredded carrots (1 lb)
fresh parsley springs, for garnish

Place crumbs and chili powder in a bag; shake to mix. Add chicken and shake to coat. Remove chicken from bag and brown in oil in large skillet over medium-high heat for 6 minutes, turning halfway through cooking. Whisk together honey mustard, milk, flour, and salt in small bowl. Arrange chicken in one side of skillet and add milk mixture to skillet along with shredded carrots. Cook over medium heat until mixture boils, stirring constantly. Distribute chicken thighs evenly over other ingredients in skillet; cover and cook 5 to 7 minutes over low heat until chicken and carrots are cooked through. Garnish with fresh parsley sprigs. Makes 4 servings.

Prayer is designed to keep us in relationship with God. . . .
Whenever you turn on the faucet to use water for cooking. . .
express a brief prayer of appreciation.
ROBERT BRYANT

**May I use those tiny kitchen tasks I do over and over
as reminders to turn my heart to You, my Lord.**

So she gleaned in the field until even.
RUTH 2:17 KJV

Let me learn from Ruth, the gleaner.
As she went out to gather the ears of corn,
so must I go forth into
the fields of prayer, meditation,
the ordinances, and hearing the word
to gather spiritual food.

CHARLES SPURGEON

BLEU CHEESE CLUB STEAKS

1 tbsp olive oil
4 club steaks (6 oz)
1 medium-size red onion,
   finely chopped
2 cloves garlic, chopped

$\frac{1}{2}$ cup beef broth
$\frac{1}{2}$ cup bottled chunky bleu cheese
   dressing
2 oz bleu cheese, crumbled

Cook steaks in oil over medium-high heat in large nonstick skillet (3 minutes per side for medium-rare, or until instant-read thermometer inserted in center registers 145°.) Remove steaks from skillet and keep warm. Sauté onion and garlic in skillet over medium heat until onion is softened. Add beef broth and cook 3 to 5 minutes, or until liquid is reduced by half. Remove skillet from heat and stir in bleu cheese dressing. Serve steaks on dinner plates and spoon equal amounts of sauce (about $\frac{1}{2}$ cup) over each steak. Crumble bleu cheese over each steak. Makes 4 servings. Serve with steak fries and fresh tossed salad.

Go, eat your food with gladness. . .
for it is now that God favors what you do.
ECCLESIASTES 9:7

Thank You, God, for Your favor.

CREAMY RICE WITH SHRIMP AND PEAS

1 (14.5-oz) can chicken broth
½ cup water
½ tsp salt
2 cups quick-cook white or
   brown rice
1 (10-oz) package frozen peas

1 (¾-lb) bag small, shelled,
   deveined, fully cooked
   shrimp
½ cup grated Parmesan cheese,
   plus more to taste

In medium-size saucepan bring broth, ½ cup water, and ½ tsp salt to a boil. Stir in rice and cover; cook over medium-low heat until tender (about 10 minutes or less). Place peas and shrimp in colander set in sink; run lukewarm water over them until thawed. Mix peas and shrimp into rice; stir in Parmesan cheese. Spoon into bowls and sprinkle with Parmesan to taste. Makes 4 servings.

Comfort thine heart with a morsel of bread. . . .
JUDGES 19:5 KJV

I'm grateful, God, for the comfort of good food.

CHICKEN AND DUMPLINGS

½ tsp salt (optional)
½ tsp pepper
1 whole chicken (3½ lbs), cut into
    8 pieces, skin removed
1 tsp vegetable oil
2½ cups buttermilk baking mix
⅔ cup milk
1 tbsp chopped parley

1 (14.5-oz) can reduced-sodium
    chicken broth
1 (10-oz) package frozen peas
    and carrots
1 (10-oz) package frozen
    whole kernel corn
1 cup frozen pearl onions

To make dumplings: Combine baking mix, milk, and parsley in bowl to make soft dough. Salt and pepper chicken; brown in oil in skillet for about 5 minutes. Combine broth and frozen vegetables with chicken in skillet. Bring to a simmer and spoon dumplings by tablespoonfuls on top. Cover and simmer 20 minutes, until chicken is tender and dumplings are cooked. Makes 8 servings.

As for the earth, out of it cometh bread.
JOB 28:5 KJV

Thank You, Lord, for earth's nourishing bounty.

Time for Jesus

That Mary. There she was again, just sitting down with the men, oblivious to the fact that there was a meal to be gotten on the table. Martha could hardly contain her frustration as she hurried around the kitchen. Here everything was ready all at the same time, the table still had to be set, and she desperately needed another pair of hands to help her. But did her sister even stick her head into the kitchen to see if Martha needed anything? No. Of course not!

When Jesus was around, Mary seemed to forget about everything else. All she wanted to do was sit at His feet and listen to Him talk. Well, Jesus' words were all well and good—Martha couldn't deny that—but the men would still expect to eat, no matter how many wise words Jesus spoke. Talk didn't fill a hungry belly—any more than it put food on the table.

Martha filled a serving bowl with vegetables and carried it to the table. She set it down with a loud thud and turned to go back to the kitchen, but the sight of Mary's serene face filled her with sudden rage. There sat Mary all calm and relaxed, while Martha was hot and tired and cross. It simply wasn't fair.

Her hands on her hips, Martha turned to the Master. "Lord, don't You even care that my sister has left me to get this meal all by myself?" The words burst out of Martha's mouth before she could stop them. "Can't You make her do her share?"

Jesus turned and looked at Martha's flushed face. For a long moment, He simply looked into her eyes, until at last she dropped her head in confusion. "Martha, Martha." He shook His head, but she heard both laughter and love in His voice. "You are worried and upset about so many things. Can't you see that only one thing really matters—and Mary has chosen that one essential thing as her focus. Meals will come and go. One day, Martha, you will see that this work that seems so important today was really a small matter. When that day comes, you may look around and wonder what to do with yourself, now that you're no longer so busy. But Mary will never lose what she has chosen."

"But. . ." The words died on Martha's lips. With tears in her eyes, she went back to the kitchen, still angry with her sister. Quietly, she finished putting the meal on the table.

After everyone had eaten, Martha stood up to clear away the food and dishes, her lips pressed tight together to keep back her resentment. But as she passed her sister, Mary reached out and tugged at her sleeve.

"Sit down, Martha," she whispered. "The dirty dishes will be here later. But Jesus won't be."

For a long moment, Martha hesitated. Then her eyes caught Jesus', and she knew He, too, was waiting for her decision. With a sigh, she sat down. Mary was right: The dishes could wait. Right now, she would make time for Jesus.

> ONE THING HAVE I DESIRED OF THE LORD, THAT WILL I SEEK AFTER; THAT I MAY DWELL IN THE HOUSE OF THE LORD ALL THE DAYS OF MY LIFE, TO BEHOLD THE BEAUTY OF THE LORD. . . .
> PSALM 27:4 KJV

SAUSAGE AND PEPPERS WITH GARLICKY MASHED POTATOES

4 medium-size potatoes (about 1½ lbs total), peeled and cut into 1-inch cubes
5 cloves garlic, peeled
1 tsp salt
1 tbsp olive oil
8 links sweet or hot Italian turkey sausages (about 1½ lbs total)

2 medium-size sweet green peppers, cored, seeded, and cut into ½-inch-thick strips
2 medium-size onions, cut into ½-inch-thick wedges

Place potatoes, 4 whole cloves garlic, and salt in medium-size saucepan; add water to cover. Bring to a boil and cook until potatoes are fork-tender (about 12 to 15 minutes). Brown sausages in oil for 3 minutes in large skillet with tight-fitting lid. Add sweet peppers and onions and cook, covered, for 5 minutes. Add 1 crushed garlic clove, increase heat to medium-high, and cook, uncovered, about 5 minutes until vegetables are browned. Remove whole garlic cloves from potato cooking liquid and place in a serving bowl; mash with back of spoon. Drain potatoes, reserving ½ cup water. Add potatoes to garlic in bowl; mash coarsely with back of spoon, adding ½ cup cooking liquid or as needed for desired consistency. Serve with sausage pieces, peppers, and onions. Makes 4 servings.

The bread is pure and fresh. The water is cool and clear.
Lord of all life, be with us, Lord of all life, be near.

AFRICAN GRACE

Be near to us, Lord, as we eat the gifts of food You have given us.

CHICKEN WITH COUSCOUS

4 boneless, skinless chicken breast
   halves (1 lb total), pounded
   ½-inch thick
4 tbsp Dijon mustard
½ cup packaged plain bread crumbs
½ lb asparagus spears, cut into
   1-inch pieces

1 (5.7-oz) box herbed
   chicken-flavor couscous
1 tsp lemon juice
½ tsp each salt, pepper
lemon wedges (optional)
4 tbsp vegetable oil

Brush each chicken breast half with 1 tablespoon mustard; coat with bread crumbs. Sauté chicken breasts in oil in skillet for 3 minutes per side over medium-high heat (or until golden). Using ½ cup more water than called for in couscous package directions, bring water to a boil. Add asparagus and cook 3 minutes, or until crisp-tender. Add couscous with remaining ingredients specified in package directions. Cover and remove from heat; let stand for 5 minutes. Stir in lemon juice, salt, and pepper. Pour onto platter and top with chicken. Garnish with lemon wedges, if desired. Makes 4 servings.

*Another glass of spilled milk! Dear Lord,
how much milk is a mother supposed to clean up in one day?
The Bible says to forgive seventy times seven.
Does that apply to spilled milk, too?*

ANITA BRYANT

Lord, please give me patience, at meal times and always.

STEAK TORTILLA ROLL-UPS

3 tbsp olive oil
1 tbsp red-wine vinegar
1½ tsp dried oregano
½ to 1 tsp chili powder

½ tsp ground cumin
1 flank steak (2 lbs)
8 flour tortillas (10-inch)
½ cup bottled salsa

Mix oil, vinegar, oregano, chili powder, and cumin in a heavy resealable plastic food-storage bag. Add steak to bag, press out air, and seal. Coat evenly and place in refrigerator overnight. Remove steak from marinade, discarding any remaining marinade. Heat broiler. Broil steak 6 inches from heat for 4 to 5 minutes per side or to desired doneness. Allow to stand for 5 minutes. Thinly slice diagonally across grain. Heat tortillas according to package directions. Spoon 1½ tablespoons salsa into each, top with meat slice, roll up, and serve. Makes 8 servings.

This is the real food of happiness: to serve one another.
ROBERT FABING

Thank You, God, for the opportunities I have to serve.

CHICKEN CHEESE STEAKS

1 large sweet red pepper, cored, seeded, cut lengthwise in 8 strips
1 onion, cut in ½-inch-thick slices
½ cup bottled Caesar dressing
4 torpedo rolls, split lengthwise

4 boneless, skinless chicken breast halves (5 oz)
1 cup shredded mozzarella cheese (about 4 oz)

Brush vegetable oil lightly over broiler-pan rack or grill rack and hinged grill basket. Heat broiler—or gas grill—to medium-hot. Toss red pepper and onion with 2 tablespoons dressing in a bowl. In another bowl, toss chicken with 2 tablespoons dressing. With flat side of meat pounder or bottom of skillet, pound chicken between sheets of plastic wrap to ½-inch thickness. Refrigerate. Broil pepper strips and onion 2 to 3 minutes per side or until tender and browned, keeping 3 to 4 inches from heat, or grill in basket 2 to 3 minutes per side. Chop vegetables coarsely and toss with remaining dressing in bowl. Unwrap chicken and broil 2 to 3 minutes per side or until no longer pink in center, keeping 3 to 4 inches from heat; cook on grill 2 minutes per side. Sprinkle ½ cup cheese on each breast. Broil or grill until cheese melts. Place chicken in rolls and spread with vegetables. Makes 4 servings.

There is no spectacle on earth more appealing than that of a beautiful woman in the act of cooking dinner for someone she loves.

THOMAS WOLFE

May I find my beauty in You, God.

Jesus did not say that the person who takes no thought for anything
in his life is blessed—no, that person is a fool.
But Jesus did teach that His disciple must make his relationship with God
the dominating focus of his life,
and to be cautiously carefree about everything else in comparison to that.
In essence, Jesus was saying,
"Don't make food and drink the controlling factor of your life,
but be focused absolutely on God."
OSWALD CHAMBERS

A Single Focus

Like Martha, so many times I let my daily responsibilities become more important than they really are. I want to get everything done right. . . . I want to be in control. . . . I want. . .well, really, what I want is for everything to go my way. I lose sight of the one thing for which my heart *truly* longs: the presence of the Lord.

I could mentally beat myself up for making this same mistake again and again—but that would be a waste of time, since it wouldn't get me back in right relation with God any quicker. No, all of us are human, and all of us are naturally sinful and selfish. The only way to counteract our natural tendencies is to simply acknowledge them, ask forgiveness, and then turn our attention back to Jesus as quickly as possible.

I can run on automatic pilot only so long, I've found. And then, when things start to fall apart and I'm forced to realize my mistake, I need to make time to simply sit at the Master's feet, regaining a healthy sense of perspective as I open my heart to His love. He is always there, whether I've lost sight of Him or not—after all, the Bible says that *nothing* can separate us from His love—but I need those quiet moments to clear my vision, so I can sense His presence once more.

In the book of Acts, Peter and John say, "We cannot but speak the things which we have seen and heard." They were referring to the gospel that they were preaching, but the same principle applies to my life. If I don't take time to sit in Jesus' presence, then what I "see and hear" will be only the world's attitudes—and that skewed perspective will come out in my speech and thoughts. But when I regularly spend time absorbing the Word, I find it reflected in my own thoughts and speech.

If I make sitting at Jesus' feet a daily habit, then I also find the rest of my routine goes that much smoother. He gives me the strength to meet my life's challenges (whether they be meeting a publisher's deadline or getting supper on the table), and often I'm surprised at the end of the day to look back and see the quiet miracles He worked throughout the busy moments. But even on the days when nothing seems to go right—when the kids quarrel, and supper is both late and burnt, and my work is going badly—I can rest in the knowledge that all Jesus asks of me is one thing: that I simply keep my focus on Him.

In matters of grace you need a daily supply.
You have no store of strength.
Day by day must you seek help from above.
It is a very sweet assurance that
a daily portion is provided for you.
In the word, through the ministry,
by meditation, in prayer, and waiting
upon God you shall receive renewed strength.
In Jesus all needful things are laid up for you.
Then enjoy your continual allowance.
Never go hungry while the daily bread of grace
is on the table of mercy.

CHARLES SPURGEON

WARM SHRIMP AND FETA SALAD

$^1/_2$ cup plus 2 tsp olive oil
3 tbsp bottled clam juice
1 tbsp lemon juice
$^1/_2$ tsp dried Italian seasoning
$^1/_2$ tsp salt
$^1/_8$ tsp pepper
1 small sweet red pepper, cored, seeded, and chopped
1 small onion, chopped

2 cloves garlic, chopped
1 sprig fresh rosemary
1 lb medium-size shrimp, cleaned and deveined
1 (6-oz) bag baby spinach leaves, cleaned and dried
10 Kalamata olives, pitted and chopped
$^1/_2$ cup crumbled flavored feta cheese (about 2 oz)

To make dressing, mix $^1/_2$ cup olive oil, clam juice, lemon juice, Italian seasoning, salt, and pepper in a small bowl. Heat remaining 2 teaspoons oil in large nonstick skillet over medium heat. Sauté red pepper, onion, garlic, and rosemary for 1 to 2 minutes or until vegetables have softened. Add shrimp and dressing to skillet and cook 3 minutes or until shrimp is pink and cooked through. Discard rosemary sprig. Toss spinach, shrimp, and dressing well in a large serving bowl. Top with Kalamata olives and feta cheese; serve warm. Makes 4 servings.

The way to a man's heart is through his stomach."
I have no doubt this is true, but it doesn't go far enough.
The way to anybody's heart is through a. . .
lovingly–presented meal. . . .
There is no greater comfort than being with those we love.
There is no reward more satisfying than creating something
with our own hands that has the power to
enhance the lives of others.
Love always begins with love.

LEO BUSCAGLIA

Fill my heart with love, Lord Jesus.

MUSTARD-CRUSTED PORK

4 boneless center-cut loin pork chops
   (1 lb total), trimmed
1 tbsp herb-flavored mustard
2 tsp olive oil

2 cloves garlic, finely chopped
2 tbsp packaged unseasoned
   bread crumbs

Heat broiler. Using meat mallet or heavy skillet, flatten chops to ½-inch thickness. Place chops on broiler-pan rack; sprinkle with salt and pepper. Combine mustard, olive oil, and garlic in small bowl; spread over chops. Sprinkle with breadcrumbs. Keeping 4 inches from heat, broil chops for 5 minutes, or until internal temperature registers 160°. Serve with broccoli and red peppers.

Breaking bread has always been seen as a form of loving,
an activity at once nurturing, life enhancing, and fun.

BIBA CAGGIANO

Lord, make all our meals nurturing. . .life enhancing. . .fun.

FUSILLI WITH CHUNKY EGGPLANT SAUCE'

1 lb fusilli
3 tbsp olive oil
1 eggplant (1 lb), cut into
   1-inch cubes

1 (28-oz) can peeled Italian
   tomatoes, undrained
½ cup coarsely chopped
   fresh basil

Cook pasta according to package directions. Drain; keep warm. In a large nonstick skillet or Dutch oven, heat olive oil over medium heat. Add eggplant and sprinkle 2 tablespoons water over top. Cover and cook 8 to 10 minutes, or until eggplant is tender. Add canned tomatoes with liquid; break up tomatoes with wooden spoon. Cover and simmer about 10 minutes. Remove from heat and stir in basil. Season with salt and pepper to taste. Turn pasta out onto serving platter and top with sauce. Makes 6 servings.

He that tilleth his land shall have plenty of bread.
PROVERBS 28:19 KJV

I'm grateful, God, for the ways You bless my hard work.

QUICK BEEF AND BARLEY SOUP

1 tbsp vegetable oil
1½ lbs boneless sirloin steak,
   cut into ½-inch cubes
1 (14.5-oz) can beef broth

½ cup quick-cook barley
5 cups water
1 (10-oz) package frozen
   mixed vegetables

Heat oil in large saucepan over medium-high heat. Separate beef into 3 batches; sauté in oil over medium-high heat, one batch at a time, for 4 minutes each. As beef browns, place in a bowl. Return all beef to saucepan and stir in broth, barley, and 5 cups of water. Bring to a boil, cover, and reduce heat; simmer for 10 minutes or until barley is tender. Stir in frozen mixed vegetables and heat through. Season with salt and pepper to taste. Makes 4 servings.

Open thine eyes, and thou shalt be satisfied with bread.
PROVERBS 20:13 KJV

**Jesus, help me not to be so busy that
I overlook the many ways You nourish me.**

Our Daily Bread

God gives me a daily portion of grace—and yet I still sometimes choose to go hungry. I suppose it's like a spiritual anorexia—an unhealthy and self-destructive refusal to nourish myself. I try to depend on my own strength—until at last I'm forced to admit I have no strength left.

Throughout all the "Juggling Our Lives" series, I'll recommend setting aside a weekly planning session for the week ahead. In this book, I've suggested that you make menus a part of that weekly plan. And I also want to recommend that you think of this weekly planning session as a time you give yourself to be alone with God. Use it as an opportunity to give each item to God (even your menus); ask for His help and wisdom as you work out the practical details of your family's life.

Having a weekly appointment with God helps me juggle my life much more smoothly. But I've also learned I need to give Him room to take me by surprise. Sometimes I pack my days so full that I leave God very little time to feed me the Bread He longs to give me. In effect, I say to Him, "Well, God, I have this little ten-minute space open today, so that would be a really good time for You to bless me, should You be so inclined, because I really don't have time for more than that." When I do that, I'm shortchanging not only God but myself. He longs for my presence—and I can't be whole without His.

Taking a long walk, soaking in a bubble bath, spending a few moments alone simply listening to music or watching the sun rise—in our busy lives, these may seem like ways to waste time. They may even seem selfish. In reality, though, we mothers need to make time for doing the things we simply enjoy. Not only do those moments refresh our bodies and emotions—those are also often the times when we notice the bread from heaven, the pieces of manna God has dropped into our lives.

As mothers, we cannot continually meet the needs of our family if we are not careful to see that our own needs are met as well. That's not being selfish. It's simply acknowledging that we aren't God.

O God, thou art my God;
early will I seek thee:
my soul thirsteth for thee,
my flesh longeth for thee. . . .
PSALM 63:1 KJV

Lord,

evermore give us this bread.

JOHN 6:34 KJV

Chicken Caesar Salad

1 tbsp vegetable oil
4 boneless, skinless chicken breast
  halves (1½ lbs total), slightly
  flattened

½ cup bottled Caesar salad dressing
1 head romaine lettuce (about 1 lb)
½ cup plain croutons

In large nonstick skillet, heat oil over medium-high heat. Sauté chicken, turning over once, until browned and no longer pink in center (about 8 to 10 minutes). Place chicken in a shallow bowl. Pour Caesar dressing over chicken, tossing to coat, and set aside. Tear romaine lettuce into bite-size pieces and place on serving plates. Cut chicken breasts diagonally into ½-inch-thick strips and arrange on top of lettuce. Top with croutons and remaining dressing. Makes 4 servings.

Thou hast given unto us for food every herb bearing seed
which is upon all the earth;
and every tree, in which is the fruit of a tree yielding seed.

Augustine

I am so glad, God, for all the ways You provide for my family.

Fajita Pitas

6 boneless, skinless chicken breast halves
1 large onion, sliced
1 large green pepper, thinly sliced
1 tbsp vegetable oil

2 cups (8-oz) shredded Mexican
   cheese blend or cheddar
   cheese
8 pita breads, halved

Sauce
1 medium onion, finely chopped
1 medium tomato, finely chopped
½ jalapeño pepper, finely chopped
guacamole and sour cream (optional)

1 tbsp minced fresh cilantro or
   parsley
1 tbsp vegetable oil

Grill chicken, covered, for 16–20 minutes over medium heat, turning occasionally, until juices run clear. Cut into strips. Sauté onion and green pepper in oil in large skillet. Add chicken and cheese. Stuff into pita halves and place on an ungreased baking sheet. Bake at 325° for 10 minutes or until cheese is melted. In a bowl, combine onion, tomato, jalapeño, cilantro, and oil in a bowl to make sauce; mix well. Serve sauce, guacamole, and sour cream, if desired, with pitas. Makes 8 servings.

I am the bread of life: he that cometh to me shall never hunger;
and he that believeth on me shall never thirst.

John 6:35 kjv

Thank You, Jesus, for meeting all my needs.

HALIBUT CHOWDER

8 to 10 green onions, thinly sliced
2 garlic cloves, minced
2 tbsp butter or margarine
4 (10¾-oz) cans condensed
    cream of potato soup, undiluted
2 (10¾-oz) cans condensed
    cream of mushroom soup,
    undiluted

4 cups milk
2 (8-oz) packages cream cheese,
    cubed
1½ lbs halibut or salmon
1½ cups frozen sliced carrots
1½ cups frozen corn
⅛ to ½ tsp cayenne pepper,
    optional

In a soup kettle, sauté onions and garlic in butter until tender. Add soups, milk, and cream cheese. Cook and stir until cheese is melted; bring to a boil. Stir in fish, carrots, and corn. Reduce heat; simmer, uncovered, for 5–10 minutes or until fish flakes easily and vegetables are tender. Add cayenne pepper if desired. Makes 16 servings.

*A meal is meant to be an event that gives us
the human experience of being our true selves in joy.
A meal is meant to re-create us.*

ROBERT FABING

Lord Jesus, give us joy in being our true selves.

ITALIAN PORK AND RICE

1 cup sliced, fresh mushrooms
1/3 cup chopped onion
1 garlic clove, minced
1 tbsp butter or margarine
1 (14½-oz) can Italian diced
   tomatoes, undrained
1 cup cubed cooked pork
   (about 2 pork chops)

½ cup chopped green pepper
½ cup chopped sweet red pepper
1 tsp Italian seasoning
½ tsp salt, optional
pinch sugar
½ cup uncooked instant rice

In a saucepan, sauté the mushrooms, onion, and garlic in butter until tender. Stir in tomatoes, pork, peppers, Italian seasoning, salt if desired, and sugar; bring to a boil. Stir in rice. Cover and remove from the heat; let stand for 5 minutes. Stir before serving. Makes 3 servings. (Double recipe if you're serving more.)

Portions of heaven are available to us for
delightful nourishment in the here and now.
In fact we can enjoy [a] feast every day.

JO KADLECEK

Thank You, God, for giving us portions of heaven every day.

101 Easy Supper Ideas

Jesus took bread, and blessed it, and brake it,
and gave it to the disciples, and said, Take, eat; this is my body.
MATTHEW 26:26 KJV

Behold, I offered Myself
wholly to the Father for you,
I even gave My whole Body and Blood for food
that I might be all yours,
and you Mine forever.

THOMAS Á KEMPIS

A Sacred Meal

As mothers, we sometimes forget that our ordinary kitchen tables are sacred places. If we think about a place being sacred at all, then many of us probably assume that the word should be reserved for churches. But in reality, I suspect God uses the conversations around our tables to build His kingdom, just as much if not more than He uses the time we spend in church. Mealtimes are special times, times when we pause in our lives long enough to communicate with God, as we thank Him for the food and our other blessings, and with each other, as we talk around the table. What's more, the Gospels tell us clearly that meals were an important part of Jesus' ministry.

So much of His ministry took place at the dinner table. He began His public life at the wedding feast in Cana; He had dinner with Levi; He fed the five thousand; He ate a Sabbath meal with the scribes and Pharisees; He went home for dinner with Zacchaeus; He was eating at a table when the woman washed His feet with her tears and her hair; and He celebrated supper with His disciples on His last night before His death. Apparently, people were so used to sitting down to a meal with Him that after the Resurrection, the disciples on the road to Emmaus were able to recognize Jesus by the characteristic way He broke the bread.

His presence makes every meal sacred.

SPEEDY SALMON PATTIES

1 (12-oz) can salmon, boned
   and skinned
$\frac{1}{3}$ cup finely chopped onion
1 egg
5 saltines, crushed

$\frac{1}{2}$ tsp Worchestershire sauce
$\frac{1}{2}$ tsp salt
$\frac{1}{8}$ tsp pepper
2 tsp butter or margarine

Combine first 7 ingredients in a bowl and mix well. Shape into six patties and fry in a skillet in butter over medium heat for 3 to 4 minutes on each side, or until heated through. Makes 3 servings. Serve with new red potatoes and green beans.

Eat ye that which is good, and let your soul delight itself in fatness.
ISAIAH 55:2 KJV

———

**Thank You, God, that You never put us on a spiritual diet.
Instead, You fill our lives with goodness.
May we always have "fat souls."**

QUICK CHICKEN CORDON BLEU

4 boneless, skinless chicken breast halves
2 tsp Dijon mustard
½ tsp paprika
4 thin slices fully cooked ham

1 cup soft bread crumbs
½ cup grated Parmesan cheese
½ tsp pepper
½ cup mayonnaise

SAUCE
1 tbsp butter or margarine
1 tbsp all-purpose flour
1 cup milk

½ tsp salt
½ cup shredded Swiss cheese
2 tbsp chicken broth

Flatten the chicken to ½-inch thickness. Spread mustard on one side; sprinkle with paprika. Top with a ham slice. Roll up tightly and secure with toothpicks. Mix breadcrumbs, Parmesan cheese, and pepper in a bowl. Brush chicken with mayonnaise and roll in crumb mixture. Place in a shallow 2-quart microwave-safe dish;

cover loosely. Microwave on high for 7 minutes. Turn chicken and cook 7 minutes longer or until juices run clear. Remove toothpicks; set aside and keep warm. In a 1-quart microwave-safe dish, heat butter on high for 30 seconds and stir in flour until smooth. Cook, uncovered, on high for 30 seconds. Add milk and salt. Cook 3–4 minutes longer or until thickened. Stir in cheese until smooth. Add broth. Serve over chicken. Makes 4 servings.

[God] never left himself without a witness;
there were always his reminders—
the kind things he did such as. . .
giving you food and gladness.
ACTS 14:17 TLB

Thank You, Lord, for Your witnesses in our lives.
Thank You for food and gladness.

PARMESAN PASTA

8 oz angel hair pasta
1 large tomato, chopped
1 (3-oz) package sliced pepperoni
1 (2½-oz) can sliced ripe olives,
   drained

½ cup grated Parmesan cheese
3 tbsp olive or vegetable oil
½ tsp salt or salt-free seasoning
   blend (optional)
½ tsp garlic powder

Cook pasta according to package directions. Combine rest of ingredients in a large serving bowl. Drain pasta; add to tomato mixture and toss to coat. Makes 4 servings.

Therefore let us keep the feast.
1 CORINTHIANS 5:8 KJV

Be always present at our feasts, Lord.

Putting Our Week in Order:

Make-Ahead Meals

Go to the ant. . .consider her ways, and be wise:
Which having no guide, overseer, or ruler,
Provideth her meat in the summer,
and gathereth her food in the harvest.

PROVERBS 6:6–8 KJV

Sometimes I'm so busy playing catch-up that I really don't have any time to plan ahead. I spend all my energy fixing yesterday's mistakes, and as a result I never have time to get ready for tomorrow. It's a little like buying things on credit; too much of my money goes toward those expensive interest payments. On the other hand, taking time to plan ahead is like a savings account for the future. It gives me greater freedom as I go through a busy week.

I've already mentioned a few ways to do this, like making a weekly schedule that includes menus. Another technique is to make use of the recipes in this chapter.

Each of the main recipes in this section is followed by recipes for two more meals from the leftovers. You may want to use these recipes on a week-by-week basis. Or as you make a habit of preparing larger meals on the weekends (or whenever you have the time), you may want to simply build up a well-stocked freezer to which you can turn throughout your week.

JUGGLING TIP:
Cook for one or two days a week on the weekend. With a little forethought, two large meals for Saturday and Sunday dinners can be used to make four more meals throughout the week.

GARLIC PORK ROAST

3½-lb pork boneless loin roast
1 tbsp vegetable oil
1 tsp salt
½ tsp pepper

1 medium onion, sliced
3 cloves garlic, peeled
1 cup chicken broth or water

Heat oil in 10-inch skillet over medium-high heat. Brown pork in oil for 10 minutes, turning occasionally. Sprinkle with salt and pepper. Place onion and garlic in 3½- to 6-quart slow cooker. Layer pork over top; then pour broth over pork. Cover and cook on low heat for 8 to 10 hours or until pork is tender.

Pork roast may also be refrigerated or frozen for use as main ingredient in other dishes. To do so, reserve 1 cup of liquid created during cooking and cool pork slightly. Shred pork with 2 forks, and place 2 cups of pork with ½ cup cooking liquid in each container. Cover and refrigerate up to 4 days, or freeze up to 4 months. Thaw by placing container in refrigerator for 8 hours. Two suggested recipes follow.

This food should be held in reserve. . .
GENESIS 41:36

Help me, Lord, to make wise plans for the days ahead.

WEEKNIGHT PORK STEW

1 container (2 cups) Garlic Pork Roast
  (previous recipe), thawed if frozen
8 small new potatoes, cut into
  $\frac{1}{2}$-inch slices
$\frac{2}{3}$ cup vegetable, chicken, or beef broth

$1\frac{1}{2}$ tsp dried basil leaves
$\frac{1}{2}$ tsp salt
1 cup frozen green peas
2 tsp cornstarch
2 tsp water

Mix first 5 ingredients in 3-quart saucepan. Bring to a boil and reduce heat. Cover and simmer 10–12 minutes or until potatoes are tender. Rinse peas with cold water to separate; stir into pork mixture. Cover and cook 2 minutes. Mix cornstarch and water; stir into pork mixture. Cook and stir 1 minute or until sauce is thickened. Makes 4 servings. Frozen corn or green beans may be substituted for peas. Serve with a crisp, green salad.

Jesus taught patience and longsuffering.
I'm sure He must have had our mealtimes in mind.

ANITA BRYANT

Jesus, give me Your spirit of patience and longsuffering—especially during mealtimes.

SPICY PORK CHILI

1 container (2 cups) Garlic Pork Roast (earlier recipe),
    thawed if frozen
2 cups hot or medium salsa
1 to 2 tsp chili powder
1 (15- or 16-oz) can pinto beans, rinsed and drained
$\frac{1}{2}$ cup shredded Colby-Monterey Jack cheese (2 oz),
    if desired
4 medium green onions, sliced ($\frac{1}{2}$ cup)
sour cream, if desired

Mix first 4 ingredients in 3-quart saucepan. Bring to a boil and reduce heat. Cover and simmer about 10 minutes or until hot. Sprinkle servings with cheese and onions; top with sour cream if desired. Serves 4. Serve with thick wedges of corn bread.

Small cheer and great welcome makes a merry feast.
WILLIAM SHAKESPEARE

Lord, may my family find all our meals a time of cheer and welcome.

Simple Feasts

Sometimes we fall into the habit of thinking of our Christian lives in spiritual terms that lack any basis in concrete reality. We forget that Jesus Himself rooted the Kingdom of God firmly in the here and now, the ordinary things we see and touch —like simple meals laid out on the kitchen table. He even went so far as to call Himself "Bread."

And if He lives in our hearts, then each time we sit down to eat with our families, we will have a feast to share.

Look simply unto Jesus for. . .food;
and what is wanted will be given,
and what is given will be blessed,
whether it be a barley grain or a wheaten loaf,
a crust or a crumb.

EDWARD M. BOUNDS

SAVORY TURKEY BREAST

6½-lb bone-in turkey breast, thawed if frozen
1 medium onion, chopped (½ cup)
1 medium stalk celery, chopped (½ cup)
1 bay leaf

1 tsp salt
½ tsp coarsely ground pepper
1 tsp chicken bouillon granules
½ cup water

Remove extra parts from cavity of turkey breast, and replace with onion, celery, and bay leaf. Place turkey in 5-quart slow cooker. Dissolve bouillon in water and pour over turkey; sprinkle with salt and pepper. Cover and cook on low for 8 to 9 hours or until juice of turkey is no longer pink when cut in center. Remove bay leaf. Serve with broccoli spears and parsley potatoes.

Or, to use turkey as a main ingredient for another dish at a later time, remove turkey from slow cooker and cool slightly. Cut up enough 1-inch pieces of turkey to make 3 full cups and place in separate refrigerator or freezer containers. May be refrigerated up to 4 days and frozen for up to 4 months. Thaw by placing in refrigerator for about 8 hours. Two suggestions follow for use in other main dishes.

I recollect with clarity the interaction of our large family. . .assembling in the dining room in eager anticipation. Our togetherness made flavors more tempting; our cozy companionship precluded loneliness. It filled our souls along with our bellies.

LEO BUSCAGLIA

———

**Tonight, Lord, as we gather around the table,
may our souls be filled as well as our stomachs.**

SWEET-AND-SOUR TURKEY

1 tbsp vegetable oil
2 medium bell peppers, cut into
   1-inch pieces
1 medium onion, cut into wedges
1 large clove garlic, finely chopped
1 container (3 cups) 1-inch pieces
   Savory Turkey Breast (previous recipe),
   thawed if frozen

½ to 1 tsp five-spice powder
1 (8-oz) can pineapple tidbits or
   chunks in juice, drained
1 (9-oz) jar sweet-and-sour
   sauce
3 cups crisp chow mein noodles

Heat oil in 12-inch skillet over medium-high heat. Stir-fry bell peppers, onion, and garlic in oil for 3–4 minutes or until crisp-tender. Add turkey and sprinkle with five-spice powder; then add pineapple and sweet-and-sour sauce. Cook about 5 minutes or until heated through, stirring occasionally. Serve over noodles or over hot cooked rice. Makes 4 to 6 servings.

When you have eaten your fill,
bless the LORD your God for the good land he has given you.
DEUTERONOMY 8:10 TLB

Thank You, God, that every night we are able to eat our fill.
Thank You for all the good things You have given us.

TURKEY BLACK BEAN WRAPS

1½ cups thick-and-chunky salsa
1 container (3 cups) shredded
   Savory Turkey Breast (earlier recipe),
   thawed if frozen
1 (15-oz) can black beans, rinsed
   and drained

1 tsp lemon or lime juice
½ to ⅓ tsp ground cumin
8 flour tortillas (8 to 10 inches
   in diameter), warmed
1½ cups shredded
   Monterey Jack cheese (6 oz)

Combine turkey, beans, salsa, lemon juice, and cumin in a 3-quart saucepan. Heat to boiling and reduce heat. Simmer for 3 to 5 minutes or until heated through. Spoon turkey mixture on tortillas, sprinkle with cheese, and roll up. Makes 8 servings.

*Cooking and caring for a family is a job that is
as dependent on the Holy Spirit as any job can be.*
ANITA BRYANT

**Help me, Lord, to rely on Your Holy Spirit
as I cook and care for my family.**

Behold, You come to me! You will to be with me!
You invite me to Your banquet!
You desire to give me heavenly food,
the Bread of Angels to eat, none other than Yourself,
the living Bread Who are come down from heaven and give life to the world.

THOMAS Á KEMPIS

Eating Stones

In the Gospels, Jesus reminds His followers that good parents don't give their children stones when they ask for bread. A lot of the time, though, I suspect I ask for stones. I think something cold and lifeless will nourish me—something like money or prestige or possessions—or a clean house or a smooth routine or a successful job—when really these things alone do my spirit as much good as it would do my body if I tried to munch a handful of gravel.

Only Jesus can really nourish my heart.

THREE-WAY BEEF

3-lb beef boneless tip roast
1 tsp salt
1 tsp mixed dried herb leaves

$\frac{1}{2}$ tsp pepper
2 cloves garlic, finely chopped
1 cup balsamic or red vinegar

Spray 12-inch skillet with cooking spray and heat over medium-high heat. Brown beef in skillet about 5 minutes; sprinkle with salt, herbs, and pepper. Place garlic in 4- to 5-quart slow cooker and layer beef over top. Pour vinegar over beef. Cover and cook on low 6 to 8 hours or until beef is tender. Pour off $\frac{1}{2}$ cup of the beef juices and set aside. Serve beef with roasted garlic mashed potatoes.

To use later in one of the two recipes that follow, slice 2 cups of beef, and along with reserved beef juice, place in refrigerator or freezer container. May be refrigerated up to 4 days and frozen up to 4 months. Thaw by placing container in refrigerator for 8 hours.

Since we all must eat, it makes sense to use these vital occasions to the maximum. It is sad to think of those who eat simply to satisfy their hunger and who do not permit themselves to linger under the many spells offered by a good meal— the satisfaction of our hearts, our minds, and our spirits.

LEO BUSCAGLIA

———————

**Tonight, dear God, as we eat our supper,
may our hearts, our minds, and our spirits be truly satisfied.**

BEEF AND BROCCOLI STIR-FRY

1 container (2 cups) Three-Way
    Beef (previous recipe), thawed
    if frozen
$\frac{1}{2}$ cup stir-fry sauce

1 (16-oz) bag frozen broccoli
    stir-fry vegetables
2 cups cooked ramen noodles
$\frac{1}{2}$ cup dry-roasted peanuts

Heat 12-inch skillet over medium-high heat. Stir-fry beef with juices, stir-fry sauce, and vegetables for 6 to 8 minutes, or until vegetables are crisp-tender. Serve mixture over noodles and sprinkle with peanuts. Serves 4.

His fruit was sweet to my taste.
SONG OF SOLOMON 2:3 KJV

———

Dear Jesus, I am grateful for all the sweetness You feed me.

101 Easy Supper Ideas

ITALIAN BEEF SANDWICHES

1 container (2 cups) Three-Way Beef (earlier recipe), thawed if frozen
6-oz sliced mozzarella or provolone cheese
1 large bell pepper, cut into rings
1 round focaccia bread (about 10 inches in diameter), cut horizontally in half

Heat beef and juices to boiling in a 2-quart saucepan. Layer beef, cheese, and bell pepper on bottom half of bread and top with remaining half. Cut into wedges. Makes 6 sandwiches.

*Here is bread, which strengthens man's heart
and is therefore called the staff of life.*
MATTHEW HENRY, 1662–1714

Strengthen our hearts, Lord.

172

In Case of Emergency:

Ground Beef and Meat Loaf Mixes

Remember that someone must cook the meals. . . .
Reflect that true humility consists in being willing and ready
to do what our Lord asks of us.

TERESA OF AVILA

No matter how much we try to work out a well-planned routine for our lives, we need to accept that sometimes even the best plans fall apart. Other times, we don't even have enough energy to make a plan, let alone carry it out. That's when it's good to have an emergency back-up.

The "mixes" in this section make good solutions to those emergency nights—or weeks—when all our regular routines aren't working. If you keep a good supply of the mix in your freezer, the recipes that follow will provide you with some options even on the busiest, most harried nights.

Keeping basic meal "mixes" always on hand in the freezer is another way to make sure you're never left in the same dilemma as Old Mother Hubbard.

JUGGLING TIP:
Make your weekly shopping list at the same time that you make your weekly schedule. Make sure to include the regular "pantry" items you use again and again (for instance, flour, milk, bread, eggs, etc.). Meal preparation is not such a challenge when you have a well-stocked kitchen.

101 Easy Supper Ideas

GROUND BEEF MIX

1 lb ground beef
½ cup chopped onion

½ cup chopped celery
½ cup chopped green pepper
(optional)

Cook ground beef and vegetables in a heavy skillet until meat is browned and vegetables are tender. Drain, cool, and freeze in 2-cup portions. Double or triple as required for any recipe calling for ground beef.

Do I live on the manna which comes down from heaven?
What is that manna but Jesus Christ Himself incarnate?

CHARLES SPURGEON

**Thank You, God,
for feeding us with the manna of Your Son.**

BEEF AND RICE

1 container Ground Beef Mix	10$\frac{1}{2}$-oz can cream of chicken soup
1$\frac{1}{2}$ cup water	10-oz package frozen peas
1 cup uncooked instant rice	$\frac{1}{2}$ tsp salt

Combine all ingredients in a large saucepan and bring to a boil. Cover and reduce heat; cook for 15 minutes. Makes approximately 6 servings.

They did eat of the fruit of the land of Canaan that year.
JOSHUA 5:12 KJV

**We are grateful, Lord,
that all year long You feed us from the fruit of the land.**

ONE-DISH DINNER

4 oz noodles
1 container Ground Beef Mix, thawed
ketchup

$10\frac{1}{2}$-oz can tomato soup
1-lb can creamed corn

Cook noodles according to package directions. In large saucepan combine ground beef, soup, and corn. When noodles are tender, drain and combine with meat mixture. Add ketchup to taste. Heat thoroughly (or bake in 350° oven for 30 to 45 minutes). Makes 6 servings.

Give us this day our daily bread.
MATTHEW 6:11 KJV

***Thank You, Heavenly Father,
that we can count on You for each day's needs.***

CHILI CASSEROLE

1 container Ground Beef Mix,
   thawed
1 pkg. chili seasoning mix
8-oz can tomato sauce
$2/3$ cup water

1-lb can kidney beans,
   undrained
4 oz corn chips
$1/2$ cup sliced, pitted black olives
grated cheese

Mix Ground Beef Mix, seasoning mix, tomato sauce, and water in a large saucepan and heat for 15 minutes. Bake in greased 9x13 casserole for 30 minutes or until cheese melts and casserole is hot. Makes approximately 8 servings.

Some of my greatest moments in life have taken place around a table of food.
JO KADLECEK

You give us so many precious moments, Lord. Thank You.

Will you take Jesus and "dwell in Him"?
See, this house is furnished with all you want,
it is filled with riches more than you will spend
as long as you live.
Here you can have intimate communion
with Christ and feast on His love;
here are tables well-stored with food
for you to live on for ever.

CHARLES SPURGEON

Our food is to feast our eyes on God.
Our meal is to commune with our God.
This is the banquet God offers us: real food.
This is the banquet meal
we are invited to attend forever.
This is eternal life.

ROBERT FABING

QUICK CHILI

1 container Ground Beef Mix,
   thawed
2 (1-lb) cans kidney beans, undrained
½ cup chopped onion
1 (32-oz) can tomatoes

1 (10½-oz) can tomato soup
½ tsp garlic powder
1½ tbsp chili powder
2 tsp salt

Combine all ingredients in a large saucepan. Cook until onions are tender and chili is hot. Makes approximately 6 servings.

We can learn the recipe for this abundant feast of love and life.
KELLY K. MONROE

**Teach me Your recipe, Lord Jesus,
for abundant love and life.**

BAKED BEANS AND HAMBURGER

1 container Ground Beef Mix,
   thawed
1 (30-oz) can pork and beans
1 (8-oz) can tomato sauce

2 tbsp vinegar
1 tsp prepared mustard
2 tbsp brown sugar

Combine ingredients in large casserole and bake at 350° for 30 minutes. Makes 6 to 8 servings.

Sometimes I get discouraged.
Help me and all women workers
The world over
To remember that you're our God
And after all is said and done,
Help us to find our rest in You.

ANONYMOUS

Remind me, God, as I work in the kitchen
that I'm not alone in this life I'm living.
We mothers are a spread-out work force,
but we're all united in love—
and we all depend on You for strength.

HAMBURGER MACARONI AND CHEESE

1 (7½-oz) package macaroni and cheese dinner
1 container Ground Beef Mix, thawed

Prepare macaroni and cheese according to package directions. Add Ground Beef Mix and heat. Makes 4–6 servings.

I am your rising bread, well kneaded
by some divine
and knotty pair of knuckles. . .
ALLA BOZARTH CAMPBELL

Dear Lord, knead me, shape me. . .
make me into bread. . .
use me to nourish others.

101 Easy Supper Ideas

A Love Feast

The next time you're rushing around trying to get supper at the same time you're doing about five other things, the next time you feel exhausted and overwhelmed and like the smallest thing might make you cry, imagine this. . .

> *Jesus comes to your door and calls your name. "Come and eat, dear one,"*
> *He says. "I have everything ready for you."*
>
> *He takes your hand and leads you gently away from your hec-*
> *tic, hurried life. You find yourself in a quiet, lovely place where a table*
> *is spread with food. Jesus holds out a chair for you. "Sit down," He says,*
> *His voice full of love. "Let Me serve you. Relax and be at peace. You*
> *and I have all the time in the world. I have everything under control."*
>
> *And so, with the tension draining from your body, you sit*
> *down and enjoy the delicious and satisfying meal He serves you. . . .*

This imaginary scene is not mere make-believe. Instead, it is reality. Jesus is waiting to serve you the Bread of Life.

Jesus saith unto them, Come and dine.
JOHN 21:12 KJV

TATER TOT CASSEROLE

1 container Ground Beef Mix, thawed
1 (10½-oz) can cream of mushroom soup
½ cup milk

½ lb tater tots
1 can french-fried onions

Cover bottom of 9x9-inch baking pan with Ground Beef Mix. Combine soup and milk in small bowl and then pour over meat mixture. Spread tater tots on top of casserole and bake at 350° for 35 minutes. Remove from oven and spread onions on top of potatoes. Return to oven and bake 10 minutes longer. Makes about 6 servings.

I am the LORD thy God. . .open thy mouth wide, and I will fill it.
PSALM 81:10 KJV

**I'm like a baby bird, Lord,
waiting with my mouth wide open for You to feed me.**

MEATLOAF MIX

1 cup milk
3 slices soft bread
½ tsp each pepper, dry mustard, sage,
   celery salt, and garlic salt

1 egg, beaten
1½ lbs ground beef
1½ tsp salt
1 tbsp Worcestershire sauce

Pour milk into large mixing bowl. Tear bread into small pieces and soak in milk. Stir in remaining ingredients and mix well. Shape into loaf and bake at 350° for 1 to 1½ hours. May be wrapped in heavy-duty foil and frozen to be baked later, or used in recipes requiring meatloaf.

*The table seems to be one of the only places left
where we willingly rest long enough to strengthen
and enliven our relationships.*

LEO BUSCAGLIA

*May we rest around the table, Lord;
may we take time to make our love for each other stronger.*

FILLED BEEF ROLL

1 Meatloaf Mix   ½ cup grated Swiss cheese
1 cup cooked rice   2 tbsp chopped green pepper

Roll thawed Meatloaf Mix into a 10x8-inch rectangle. Combine rice, cheese, and green pepper in small bowl. Pat rice mixture onto meatloaf, leaving 1-inch margins all round. Roll up jellyroll style and seal side ends and seams by pressing meat edges together. Bake at 350° for 35 minutes. Makes 8 servings.

*The resurrection of the Lord is revealed to the apostles
and those who were with them while they were "at table."
In the context of a meal Jesus appeared and showed himself
as the one who has power over death.*

ROBERT FABING

**Lord, reveal to us Your resurrection tonight
as we eat together.**

CHEESE MEATLOAF

1 Meatloaf Mix, thawed
½ lb grated cheddar or crumbled
    bleu cheese

1 egg white
1 tbsp water
2 slices bread

Press half of Meatloaf Mix into a greased 9x5x3-inch pan. Mix slightly beaten egg white and water. Toss torn bread pieces with egg white and water. Add cheese and toss gently. Cover meat with cheese mixture; top with rest of meat. Bake at 350° for 1½ hours. Makes 6 servings.

What man is there of you, whom if his son ask bread,
will he give him a stone?
MATTHEW 7:9 KJV

You know how I love to give my children
that which makes them happy.
Thank You for loving each of us still more
than any mother loves.
Thank You for all the ways You nourish and delight us.

MEATBALLS

Shape Meat Loaf mix into balls and fry in olive oil or bake at 350° for 10–15 minutes until browned. Four pounds of Meatloaf Mix will make about 12 dozen meatballs. Freeze and keep on hand to add to tomato sauce for spaghetti or use in the recipe that follows.

My beloved is mine, and I am his: he feedeth among the lilies.
SONG OF SOLOMON 2:16 KJV

Beloved Lord, thank You that You and I belong to each other.

MEATBALL STROGANOFF

1 cup chopped onion
$\frac{1}{2}$ cup butter
3 tbsp flour
$\frac{1}{8}$ tsp garlic powder
$\frac{1}{8}$ tsp pepper

1 tbsp ketchup
1 ($10\frac{1}{2}$-oz) can condensed beef bouillon
$\frac{1}{2}$ cup water
30 meatballs
$1\frac{1}{2}$ cup sour cream

In large saucepan, cook onion in butter until tender. Stir in flour; add garlic powder, pepper, ketchup, bouillon, and water. Cook and stir until mixture bubbles. Add meatballs and cook over low heat—10 minutes for thawed meatballs, 20 minutes for frozen. Stir occasionally. Mix in sour cream and heat, but do not allow to boil. Serve over rice or noodles. Makes about 6–8 servings.

The fruit of the Spirit is in all goodness and righteousness and truth.
EPHESIANS 5:9 KJV

Holy Spirit, may my life bear a bountiful crop of nourishing fruit.

Come to the Table

A few years ago, I made a wall hanging for a friend of mine that showed an angel flying through the stars with her bright hair sweeping out behind her. With gold embroidery floss, I stitched these words on the black sky: *Angels fly because they take themselves lightly.* I knew that, like me, my friend was often burdened with responsibilities. Too often, we both took our various jobs so seriously that we plodded through life, far too weighted down to fly with the angels.

As you juggle your family's meals along with all your other busy responsibilities, remember—the world will not end if this ball gets dropped now and then. The word "juggle" comes from the Latin word for "jest"; in other words, juggling is a joke, a game. We need to be like children again, finding the simple pleasures and silly joys that are scattered throughout our lives. We need to not take ourselves so seriously.

My children love to make things in the kitchen. They love to pour and sift and beat and shake. The mess doesn't bother them; the success or failure of their efforts has little importance to them. They're simply having fun.

Cooking *is* fun. Eating is fun. Even cleaning up can be fun when we remember we are all guests at an eternal banquet of love.

I am His guest, and He my living food.
FRANCIS QUARLES

Ellyn Sanna, wife, mother, and expert "juggler" is the author of more than twenty books, including *By the Water* (Promise Press, April 2000). She speaks at women's retreats and mothers' groups and works as a full-time freelance editor. She and her family make their home in upstate New York.

Coming Soon for Fall 2001!

**101 Time-Management Tips
for Busy Moms**
ISBN: 1-58660-208-X

**101 Ways to Improve
Your Marriage**
ISBN: 1-58660-207-1

Paperback • 192 pages • $8.99